# TEACHER'S PET PUBLICATIONS

LITPLAN TEACHER PACK
for
Macbeth

based on the book by
William Shakespeare

Written by
Mary B. Collins

© 1996 Teacher's Pet Publications
All Rights Reserved

This **LitPlan** for William Shakespeare's
Macbeth
has been brought to you by Teacher's Pet Publications, Inc.

Copyright Teacher's Pet Publications 1996
11504 Hammock Point
Berlin MD 21811

Only the student materials in this unit plan may be reproduced. Pages such as worksheets and study guides may be reproduced for use in the purchaser's classroom. For any additional copyright questions, contact Teacher's Pet Publications.

TABLE OF CONTENTS - *Macbeth*

Introduction	10
Unit Objectives	12
Reading Assignment Sheet	13
Unit Outline	14
Study Questions (Short Answer)	21
Quiz/Study Questions (Multiple Choice)	30
Pre-reading Vocabulary Worksheets	45
Lesson One (Introductory Lesson)	57
Nonfiction Assignment Sheet	60
Oral Reading Evaluation Form	64
Writing Assignment 1	66
Writing Assignment 2	72
Writing Assignment 3	83
Writing Evaluation Form	73
Vocabulary Review Activities	71
Extra Writing Assignments/Discussion ?s	76
Unit Review Activities	85
Unit Tests	89
Unit Resource Materials	131
Vocabulary Resource Materials	147

ABOUT THE AUTHOR
WILLIAM SHAKESPEARE

SHAKESPEARE, William (1564-1616). For more than 350 years, William Shakespeare has been the world's most popular playwright. On the stage, in the movies, and on television his plays are watched by vast audiences. People read his plays again and again for pleasure. Students reading his plays for the first time are delighted by what they find.

Shakespeare's continued popularity is due to many things. His plays are filled with action, his characters are believable, and his language is thrilling to hear or read. Underlying all this is Shakespeare's deep humanity. He was a profound student of people and he understood them. He had a great tolerance, sympathy, and love for all people, good or evil.

While watching a Shakespearean tragedy, the audience is moved and shaken. After the show the spectators are calm, washed clean of pity and terror. They are saddened but at peace, repeating the old saying, "There, but for the grace of God, go I."

A Shakespearean comedy is full of fun. The characters are lively; the dialogue is witty. In the end young lovers are wed; old babblers are silenced; wise men are content. The comedies are joyous and romantic.

Boyhood in Stratford

William Shakespeare was born in Stratford-upon-Avon, England, in 1564. This was the sixth year of the reign of Queen Elizabeth I. He was christened on April 26 of that year. The day of his birth is unknown. It has long been celebrated on April 23, the feast of St. George.

He was the third child and oldest son of John and Mary Arden Shakespeare. Two sisters, Joan and Margaret, died before he was born. The other children were Gilbert, a second Joan, Anne, Richard, and Edmund. Only the second Joan outlived William.

Shakespeare's father was a tanner and glovemaker. He was an alderman of Stratford for years. He also served a term as high bailiff, or mayor. Toward the end of his life John Shakespeare lost most of his money. When he died in 1601, he left William only a little real estate. Not much is known about Mary Shakespeare, except that she came from a wealthier family than her husband.

Stratford-upon-Avon is in Warwickshire, called the heart of England. In Shakespeare's day it was well farmed and heavily wooded. The town itself was prosperous and progressive.

The town was proud of its grammar school. Young Shakespeare went to it, although when or for how long is not known. He may have been a pupil there between his 7th and 13th years. His studies must have been mainly in Latin. The schooling was good. All four schoolmasters at the school during Shakespeare's boyhood were graduates of Oxford University.

Nothing definite is known about his boyhood. From the content of his plays, he must have learned early about the woods and fields, about birds, insects, and small animals, about trades and outdoor sports, and about the country people he later portrayed with such good humor. Then and later he picked up an amazing stock of facts about hunting, hawking, fishing, dances, music, and other arts and sports. Among other subjects, he also learned about alchemy, astrology, folklore, medicine, and law. As good writers do, he collected information both from books and from daily observation of the world around him.

Marriage and Life in London

In 1582, when he was 18, he married Anne Hathaway. She was from Shottery, a village a mile from Stratford. Anne was seven or eight years older than Shakespeare. From this difference in their ages, a story arose that they were unhappy together. Their first daughter, Susanna, was born in 1583. In 1585 a twin boy and girl, Hamnet and Judith, were born.

What Shakespeare did between 1583 and 1592 is not known. Various stories are told. He may have taught school, worked in a lawyer's office, served on a rich man's estate, or traveled with a company of actors. One famous story says that about 1584 he and some friends were caught poaching on the estate of Sir Thomas Lucy of Carlecote, near Warwick, and were forced to leave town. A less likely story is that he was in London in 1588. There he was supposed to have held horses for theater patrons and later to have worked in the theaters as a callboy.

By 1592, however, Shakespeare was definitely in London and was already recognized as an actor and playwright. He was then 28 years old. In that year he was referred to in another man's book for the first time. Robert Greene, a playwright, accused him of borrowing from the plays of others.

Between 1592 and 1594, plague kept the London theaters closed most of the time. During these years Shakespeare wrote his earliest sonnets and two long narrative poems, 'Venus and Adonis' and 'The Rape of Lucrece'. Both were printed by Richard Field, a boyhood friend from Stratford. They were well received and helped establish him as a poet.

Shakespeare Prospers

Until 1598 Shakespeare's theater work was confined to a district northeast of London. This was outside the walls, in the parish of Shoreditch. Located there were two playhouses, the Theatre and the Curtain. Both were managed by James Burbage, whose son Richard Burbage was Shakespeare's friend and the greatest tragic actor of his day.

Up to 1596 Shakespeare lived near these theaters in Bishopsgate, where the North Road entered the city. Sometime between 1596 and 1599, he moved across the Thames River to a district called Bankside. There, two theaters, the Rose and the Swan, had been built by Philip Henslowe. He was James Burbage's chief competitor in London as a theater manager.

The Burbages also moved to this district in 1598 and built the famous Globe Theatre. Its sign showed Atlas supporting the world-hence the theater's name. Shakespeare was associated with the Globe Theatre for the rest of his active life. He owned shares in it, which brought him much money.

Meanwhile, in 1597, Shakespeare had bought New Place, the largest house in Stratford. During the next three years he bought other property in Stratford and in London. The year before, his father, probably at Shakespeare's suggestion, applied for and was granted a coat of arms. It bore the motto Non sanz droict-Not without right. From this time on, Shakespeare could write "Gentleman" after his name. This meant much to him, for in his day actors were classed legally with criminals and vagrants.

Shakespeare's name first appeared on the title pages of his printed plays in 1598. In the same year Francis Meres, in 'Palladis Tamia: Wit's Treasury', praised him as a poet and dramatist. Meres's comments on 12 of Shakespeare's plays showed that Shakespeare's genius was recognized in his own time.

Honored As Actor and Playwright

Queen Elizabeth I died in 1603. King James I followed her to the throne. Shakespeare's theatrical company was taken under the king's patronage and called the King's Company. Shakespeare and the other actors were made officers of the royal household. The theatrical company was the most successful of its time. Before it was the King's Company, it had been known as the Earl of Derby's and the Lord Chamberlain's. In 1608 the company acquired the Blackfriars Theatre. This was a smaller and more aristocratic theater than the Globe. Thereafter the company alternated between the two playhouses.

Plays by Shakespeare were performed at both theaters, at the royal court, and in the castles of the nobles. After 1603 Shakespeare probably acted little, although he was still a good actor. His favorite roles seem to have been old Adam in 'As You Like It' and the Ghost in 'Hamlet'.

In 1607, when he was 43, he may have suffered a serious physical breakdown. In the same year his older daughter Susanna married John Hall, a doctor. The next year Shakespeare's first grandchild, Elizabeth, was born. Also in 1607 his brother Edmund, who had been an actor in London, died at the age of 27.

The Mermaid Tavern Group

About this time Shakespeare became one of the group of now-famous writers who gathered at the Mermaid Tavern in Cheapside. The club was formed by Sir Walter Raleigh. Ben Jonson was its leading spirit (see Jonson). Shakespeare was a popular member. He was admired for his talent and loved for his kindliness. Thomas Fuller, writing about 50 years later, gave an amusing account of the conversational duels between Shakespeare and Jonson:

"Many were the wit-combats betwixt him and Ben Jonson; which two I behold like a Spanish great galleon and an English man-of-war; Master Jonson (like the former) was built far higher in learning; solid, but slow, in his performances. Shakespeare, with the English man-of-war, lesser in bulk, but lighter in sailing, could turn with all tides, tack about, and take advantage of all winds, by the quickness of his wit and invention."

Jonson sometimes criticized Shakespeare harshly. Nevertheless he later wrote a eulogy of Shakespeare that is remarkable for its feeling and acuteness. In it he said:

> Leave thee alone, for the comparison
> Of all that insolent Greece or haughty Rome
> Sent forth, or since did from their ashes come.
> Triumph, my Britain, thou hast one to show
> To whom all scenes of Europe homage owe.
> He was not of an age, but for all time!
> . . . .
> Sweet Swan of Avon! what a sight it were
> To see thee in our waters yet appear,
> And make those flights upon the banks of Thames,
> That so did take Eliza, and our James!

Death and Burial at Stratford

Shakespeare retired from his theater work in 1610 and returned to Stratford. His friends from London visited him. In 1613 the Globe Theatre burned. He lost much money in it, but he was still wealthy. He shared in the building of the new Globe. A few months before the fire he bought as an investment a house in the fashionable Blackfriars district of London.

On April 23, 1616, Shakespeare died at the age of 52. This date is according to the Old Style, or Julian, calendar of his time. The New Style, or Gregorian, calendar date is May 3, 1616. He was buried in the chancel of the Church of the Holy Trinity in Stratford.

A stone slab-a reproduction of the original one, which it replaced in 1830-marks his grave. It bears an inscription, perhaps written by himself.

On the north wall of the chancel is his monument. It consists of a portrait bust enclosed in a stone frame. Below it is an inscription in Latin and English. This bust and the engraving by Martin Droeshout, prefixed to the First Folio edition of his plays (1623), are the only pictures of Shakespeare which can be accepted as showing his true likeness.

John Aubrey, an English antiquarian, wrote about Shakespeare 65 years after the poet's death. He evidently used information furnished by the son of one of Shakespeare's fellow actors. Aubrey described him as "a handsome, well-shaped man, very good company, and of a ready and pleasant smooth wit."

Shakespeare's will, still in existence, bequeathed most of his property to Susanna and her daughter. He left small mementoes to friends. He mentioned his wife only once, leaving her his "second best bed" with its furnishings.

Much has been written about this odd bequest. There is little reason to think it was a slight. Indeed, it may have been a special mark of affection. The "second best bed" was probably the one they used. The best bed was reserved for guests. At any rate, his wife was entitled by law to one third of her husband's goods and real estate and to the use of their home for life. She died in 1623.

The will contains three signatures of Shakespeare. These, with three others, are the only known specimens of his handwriting in existence. Several experts also regard some lines in the manuscript of 'Sir Thomas More' as Shakespeare's own handwriting. He spelled his name in
various ways. His father's papers show about 16 spellings. Shakspere, Shaxpere, and Shakespeare are the most common.

Did Shakespeare Really Write the Plays?

The outward events of Shakespeare's life are ordinary. He was hard-working, sober, and middle-class in his ways. He steadily gathered wealth and took good care of his family. Many people have found it impossible to believe that such a man could have written the plays. They feel that he could not have known such heights and depths of passion. They believe that the people around Shakespeare expressed little realization of his greatness. Some say that a man of his little schooling could not have learned about the professions, the aristocratic sports of hawking and hunting, the speech and manners of the upper classes.

Since the 1800's there has been a steady effort to prove that Shakespeare did not write the plays or that others did. For a long time the leading candidate was Sir Francis Bacon. Books on the

Shakespeare-Bacon argument would fill a library (see Bacon, Francis). After Bacon became less popular, the Earl of Oxford and then other men were suggested as the authors. Nearly every famous Elizabethan was named. The most recent has been Christopher Marlowe. Some people even claim that "Shakespeare" is an assumed name for a whole group of poets and playwrights.

However, some men around Shakespeare-for example, Meres in 1598 and Jonson in 1623-did recognize his worth as a man and as a writer. To argue that an obscure Stratford boy could not have become the Shakespeare of literature is to ignore the mystery of genius. His knowledge
is of the kind that could not be learned in school. It is the kind that only a genius could learn, by applying a keen intelligence to everyday life. Some great writers have had even less schooling than Shakespeare.

Few scholars take seriously these attempts to deprive Shakespeare of credit. Shakespeare's style is individual and cannot be imitated. Any good student recognizes it. It can be found nowhere else. Bacon is a poor candidate for the honor. Great as he was, he was certainly not a poet.

How the Plays Came Down to Us

Since the 1700's scholars have worked over the text of Shakespeare's plays. They have had to do so because the plays were badly printed, and no original manuscripts of them survive.

In Shakespeare's day plays were not usually printed under the author's supervision. When a playwright sold a play to his company, he lost all rights to it. He could not sell it again to a publisher without the company's consent. When the play was no longer in demand on the
stage, the company itself might sell the manuscript. Plays were eagerly read by the Elizabethan public. This was even more true during the plague years, when the theaters were closed. It was also true during times of business depression. Sometimes plays were taken down in
shorthand and sold. At other times, a dismissed actor would write down the play from memory and sell it.

About half of Shakespeare's plays were printed during his lifetime in small, cheap pamphlets called quartos. Most of these were made from fairly accurate manuscripts. A few were in garbled form.

In 1623, seven years after Shakespeare's death, his collected plays were published in a large, expensive volume called the First Folio. It contains all his plays except two of which he wrote only part-'Pericles' and 'Two Noble Kinsmen'. It also has the first engraved portrait of
Shakespeare.

This edition was authorized by Shakespeare's acting group, the King's Company. Some of the plays in it were printed from the accurate quartos and some from manuscripts in the theater. It is certain that many of these manuscripts were in Shakespeare's own handwriting. Others were copies. Still others, like the 'Macbeth' manuscript, had been revised by another dramatist.

Shakespearean scholars have been determining what Shakespeare actually wrote. They have done so by studying the language, stagecraft, handwriting, and printing of the period and by carefully examining and comparing the different editions. They have modernized spelling and punctuation, supplied stage directions, explained difficult passages, and made the plays easier for the modern reader to understand.

Another hard task has been to find out when the plays were written. About half of them have no definite date of composition. The plays themselves have been searched for clues. Other books have been examined. Scholars have tried to match events in Shakespeare's life with the subject matter of his plays.

These scholars have used detective methods. They have worked with clues, deduction, shrewd reasoning, and external and internal evidence. External evidence consists of actual references in other books. Internal evidence is made up of verse tests and a study of the poet's imagery and figures of speech, which changed from year to year.

The verse tests follow the idea that a poet becomes more skillful with practice. Scholars long ago noticed that in his early plays Shakespeare used little prose, much rhyme, and certain types of rhythmical and metrical regularity. As he grew older he used more prose, less rhyme, and greater freedom and variety in rhythm and meter. From these facts, scholars have figured out the dates of those plays that had none.

Shakespeare As a Dramatist

The facts about Shakespeare are interesting in themselves, but they have little to do with his place in literature. Shakespeare wrote his plays to give pleasure. It is possible to spoil that pleasure by giving too much attention to his life, his times, and the problem of figuring out what he actually wrote. He can be enjoyed in book form, in the theater, or on television without our knowing any of these things.

Some difficulties stand in the way of this enjoyment. Shakespeare wrote more than 350 years ago. The language he used is naturally somewhat different from the language of today. Besides, he wrote in verse. Verse permits a free use of words that may not be understood by some readers. His plays are often fanciful. This may not appeal to matter-of-fact people who are used to modern realism. For all these reasons, readers may find him difficult. The worst handicap to enjoyment is the notion that Shakespeare is a "classic," a writer to be approached with awe.

The way to escape this last difficulty is to remember that Shakespeare wrote his plays for everyday people and that many in the audience were uneducated. They looked upon him as a funny, exciting, and lovable entertainer, not as a great poet. People today should read him as the people in his day listened to him. The excitement and enjoyment of the plays will banish most of the difficulties.

--- Courtesy of Compton's Learning Company

INTRODUCTION

This unit has been designed to develop students' reading, writing, thinking, and language skills through exercises and activities related to *Macbeth* by William Shakespeare. It includes twenty-four lessons, supported by extra resource materials.

The **introductory lesson** introduces students to Shakespeare and his times through a group research project. Following the introductory activity, students are given a transition to explain how the activity relates to the play they are about to read. Following the transition, students are given the materials they will be using during the unit. At the end of the lesson, students begin the pre-reading work for the first reading assignment.

The **reading assignments** are approximately thirty pages each; some are a little shorter while others are a little longer. Students have approximately 15 minutes of pre-reading work to do prior to each reading assignment. This pre-reading work involves reviewing the study questions for the assignment and doing some vocabulary work for some challenging vocabulary words they will encounter in their reading.

The **study guide questions** are fact-based questions; students can find the answers to these questions right in the text. These questions come in two formats: short answer or multiple choice. The best use of these materials is probably to use the short answer version of the questions as study guides for students (since answers will be more complete), and to use the multiple choice version for occasional quizzes. If your school has the appropriate equipment, it might be a good idea to make transparencies of your answer keys for the overhead projector.

The **vocabulary work** is intended to enrich students' vocabularies as well as to aid in the students' understanding of the play. Prior to each reading assignment, students will complete a two-part worksheet for approximately 10 vocabulary words in the upcoming reading assignment. Part I focuses on students' use of general knowledge and contextual clues by giving the sentence in which the word appears in the text. Students are then to write down what they think the words mean based on the words' usage. Part II nails down the definitions of the words by giving students dictionary definitions of the words and having students match the words to the correct definitions based on the words' contextual usage. Students should then have an understanding of the words when they meet them in the text.

After each reading assignment, students will go back and formulate answers for the study guide questions. Discussion of these questions serves as a **review** of the most important events and ideas presented in the reading assignments.

After students complete reading the work, there is a **vocabulary review** lesson which pulls together all of the fragmented vocabulary lists for the reading assignments and gives students a review of all of the words they have studied.

Following the vocabulary review, a lesson is devoted to the **extra discussion questions/writing assignments**. These questions focus on interpretation, critical analysis and personal response, employing a variety of thinking skills and adding to the students' understanding of the play.

The **project** which follows the discussion questions deals with people who have been assassinated throughout history and focuses on how the assassinations affected the people of the country/world.

There are three **writing assignments** in this unit, each with the purpose of informing, persuading, or having students express personal opinions. The first assignment is to inform: students take the information they have gathered through research, group work and class discussion and organize it into a composition. The second assignment is to persuade: students attempt to persuade Macbeth not to kill Duncan. The third assignment is to give students the opportunity to be creative and express their own opinions: students rewrite the plot of *Macbeth* from Lady Macbeth's point of view in the first person narrative.

In addition, there is a **nonfiction reading assignment**. Students are required to read a piece of nonfiction related in some way to *Macbeth*. After reading their nonfiction pieces, students will fill out a worksheet on which they answer questions regarding facts, interpretation, criticism, and personal opinions. During one class period, students make **oral presentations** about the nonfiction pieces they have read. This not only exposes all students to a wealth of information, it also gives students the opportunity to practice **public speaking**. This nonfiction assignment is done in conjunction with the introductory research assignment.

The **review lesson** pulls together all of the aspects of the unit. The teacher is given four or five choices of activities or games to use which all serve the same basic function of reviewing all of the information presented in the unit.

The **unit test** comes in two formats: all multiple choice-matching-true/false or with a mixture of matching, short answer, multiple choice, and composition. As a convenience, two different tests for each format have been included. There is also an advanced short answer version of the unit test.

There are additional **support materials** included with this unit. The **extra activities packet** includes suggestions for an in-class library, crossword and word search puzzles related to the play, and extra vocabulary worksheets. There is a list of **bulletin board ideas** which gives the teacher suggestions for bulletin boards to go along with this unit. In addition, there is a list of **extra class activities** the teacher could choose from to enhance the unit or as a substitution for an exercise the teacher might feel is inappropriate for his/her class. **Answer keys** are located directly after the **reproducible student materials** throughout the unit. The student materials may be reproduced for use in the teacher's classroom without infringement of copyrights. No other portion of this unit may be reproduced without the written consent of Teacher's Pet Publications.

UNIT OBJECTIVES - *Macbeth*

1. Through reading Shakespeare's *Macbeth* students will gain a better understanding of the traditional theme of good vs. evil.

2. Students will demonstrate their understanding of the text on four levels: factual, interpretive, critical and personal.

3. Students will analyze characters to better understand motivation for action.

4. As they are exposed to the path of the main character's personal development (or perhaps degeneration), students will see the consequences of greed.

5. Students will learn that political struggles for power within a government are a part of any historical era, not just modern times.

6. Students will be exposed to background information about Shakespeare, Elizabethan drama, and *Macbeth*.

7. Students will examine Shakespeare's use of language.

8. Students will be given the opportunity to practice reading aloud and silently to improve their skills in each area.

9. Students will answer questions to demonstrate their knowledge and understanding of the main events and characters in *Macbeth* as they relate to the author's theme development.

10. Students will enrich their vocabularies and improve their understanding of the play through the vocabulary lessons prepared for use in conjunction with the play.

11. The writing assignments in this unit are geared to several purposes:
    a. To have students demonstrate their abilities to inform, to persuade, or to express their own personal ideas
        Note: Students will demonstrate ability to write effectively to <u>inform</u> by developing and organizing facts to convey information. Students will demonstrate the ability to write effectively to <u>persuade</u> by selecting and organizing relevant information, establishing an argumentative purpose, and by designing an appropriate strategy for an identified audience. Students will demonstrate the ability to write effectively to <u>express personal ideas</u> by selecting a form and its appropriate elements.
    b. To check the students' reading comprehension
    c. To make students think about the ideas presented by the play

READING ASSIGNMENT SHEET - *Macbeth*

Date Assigned	Reading Assignment Act: Scene(s)	Completion Date
	I: i, ii, iii, iv	
	I: v, vi, vii	
	II: i, ii, iii, iv	
	III: i, ii, iii, iv	
	III: v, vi IV: i, ii	
	IV: iii V: i, ii, iii	
	V: iv, v, vi, vii	

UNIT OUTLINE - *Macbeth*

1 Library	2 Nonfiction Reports	3 Materials Parts PV Act I	4 Read Act I	5 Read Act I
6 Study ?s Act I Parts Act II PV Act II	7 Read Act II	8 Writing Assignment 1	9 Study ?s Act II Parts Act III PV Act III	10 Read Act III
11 Read Act III	12 Study ?s Act III Parts Act IV PV Act IV	13 Read Act IV	14 Study ?s Act IV Parts Act V PV Act V	15 Read Act V
16 Study ?s Act V Vocabulary	17 Writing Assignment 2	18 Project	19 Project	20 Extra Questions
21 Writing Assignment 3	22 Film	23 Review	24 Test	

Key: P = Preview Study Questions   V = Vocabulary Work   R = Read

SUMMARY - *Macbeth*

I.i: Three witches meet and decide when to meet again. "Fair is foul and foul is fair"

I.ii: A soldier reports to Duncan that Macbeth killed Macdonwald -- Macbeth and Banquo joined forces to defeat Thane of Cawdor and King of Norway -- Duncan decides to give the Thane of Cawdor's title to Macbeth

I.iii: Witches meet again -- Call Macbeth Thane of Glamis, Thane of Cawdor and king hereafter, foretelling his rise to power -- Macbeth learns that Duncan has given him the title of Thane of Cawdor -- Macbeth wonders if the witches' predictions of his becoming king will come true

I.iv: Malcolm describes Cawdor's death to Duncan -- Duncan promises Banquo rewards for his services -- Duncan proclaims Malcolm his successor -- Duncan announces his intentions to visit Macbeth at Inverness, Macbeth's castle

I.v: Lady Macbeth reads a letter from Macbeth describing the witches' prophecy -- A messenger tells her of Duncan's visit, and she decides she will have to help Macbeth kill Duncan that night

I.vi: Lady Macbeth welcomes Duncan and his party cordially and makes the king feel comfortable

I.vii: Macbeth tries to decide whether or not to kill Duncan -- Lady Macbeth enters and bullies him into deciding to kill Duncan

II.i: Banquo tells Fleance of his fears about the witches' predictions -- Macbeth enters and lies, saying he doesn't think about it -- Macbeth, alone, has a vision of a bloody dagger and again has second thought about killing Duncan

II.ii: Lady Macbeth does her part (drugs the king's guards) -- Macbeth kills Duncan but forgets to leave the daggers at the scene -- He won't go back, so Lady Macbeth takes the daggers back and fixes the scene of the crime to look like the guards killed the king

II.iii: Macduff and Lennox come to Inverness to wake the king -- The murder is discovered -- In his acted grief and rage, Macbeth kills the two guards, whom he had framed for the murder -- Malcolm and Donalbain flee the country -- Banquo enters and says he suspects treason

II.iv: Macduff, Ross and an old man tell the theories of who murdered the king -- One theory is that the guards did it -- Another theory is that the king's sons are suspected, since they have fled -- Ross doesn't believe this theory is possible -- Macduff tells that Macbeth's coronation is scheduled

III.i: Banquo suspects Macbeth had something to do with the king's murder -- Macbeth decides to get rid of Banquo and Fleance and gets two convicted murderers to do it for him

Macbeth Plot Summary Page 2

III.ii: Lady Macbeth tries to get Macbeth to act other than how he feels -- Macbeth hints to her of Banquo's death, but spares her actual knowledge

III.iii: The murderers kill Banquo, but Fleance escapes

III.iv: One murderer reports to Macbeth that Banquo is dead and Fleance escaped -- As Macbeth goes to sit at the banquet table, Banquo's ghost appears to him -- Macbeth loses control and almost tells that he is responsible for murder -- Lady Macbeth tries to cover for him and gets rid of the guests -- Macbeth reveals he will see the witches again, and he realizes that he can't turn back, he can only go forward

III.v: Hecate tells the witches what to do at their meeting with Macbeth

III.vi: We learn that Macduff has gone to England to help Malcolm

IV.i: The witches, through visions, show Macbeth that he should beware of Macduff, that no one "born of woman" can harm him, that no one shall vanquish him "until Birnam Wood moves to Dunsinane Hill," and finally, that Banquo's descendants will be kings -- Macbeth decides to kill Macduff's family and servants

IV.ii: Lady Macduff is upset at Macduff's leaving them so suddenly -- A messenger comes to warn her to leave her home, but he is too late -- The men Macbeth sent came and killed her, her son and the servants

IV.iii: Malcolm tests Macduff by telling him that he (Malcolm) would be an even more bloodthirsty tyrant than Macbeth -- Macduff is disheartened and begins to leave, thus passing Malcolm's test -- They decide to fight together against Macbeth -- Ross enters and tells Macduff his family has been killed

V.i: Lady Macbeth's servant shows the doctor Lady Macbeth sleepwalking -- In her sleep, she talks about Duncan's murder, Macduff's wife's murder and Banquo's burial -- The doctor tells the servant to watch Lady Macbeth, foreshadowing her suicide

V.ii: The armies gather near Dunsinane to group for their attack on Macbeth -- We learn that Macbeth's army and servants are no longer loyal

V.iii: Macbeth prepares for battle and sends Seyton to hang anyone in his army who appears not to be loyal -- The doctor tells Macbeth that his wife's troubles are psychological, not physical

V.iv: We see how soon "Birnam Wood will move to Dunsinane" as Malcolm has his soldiers use cut tree branches to hide

Macbeth Plot Summary Page 3

V.v: Macbeth gets two major pieces of bad news: Lady Macbeth is dead and Birnam Wood is moving towards Dunsinane

V.vi: Malcolm has his soldiers drop their cover, and he, Siward and Macduff get ready for their attack on Macbeth

V.vii: Macbeth kills Young Siward -- Malcolm and Siward say the castle will be easily taken since Macbeth's army is not particularly loyal

V.viii: Macbeth and Macduff meet -- Macbeth doesn't want to fight, but Macduff forces him to -- Macduff wins, beheading Macbeth -- Old Siward learns of his son's death, and, although sad, praises his son's courage -- Malcolm regains the throne

STUDY GUIDE QUESTIONS

SHORT ANSWER STUDY GUIDE QUESTIONS - *Macbeth*

Act One

1. What is the point of the first scene literally and in reference to the whole play?
2. What does Duncan call Macbeth when he hears Macbeth has defeated Macdonwald?
3. Who is sentenced to death?
4. What do the witches predict in I.iii for Macbeth? For Banquo?
5. What news does Ross bring Macbeth?
6. Banquo, like Macbeth, is surprised that the witches have predicted Macbeth's new title. He is, however, leery. What does he say about the motives of the "instruments of darkness"?
7. Malcolm describes Cawdor's last moments before execution. What is Duncan's reply?
8. Macbeth says, "Stars, hide your fires, Let not light see my black and deep desires." What are Macbeth's desires?
9. After Lady Macbeth reads the letter, what does she tell us is her opinion of Macbeth, and how does she plan to help him?
10. What is Lady Macbeth's "prayer" to the spirits after she learns Duncan is coming"?
11. What advice does Lady Macbeth give Macbeth when he arrives home?
12. What are Macbeth's arguments to himself against killing Duncan?
13. What arguments does Lady Macbeth use to convince Macbeth to commit the murder?
14. What is Lady Macbeth's plan?

Act II

1. What is Macbeth's lie to Banquo about the witches' predictions?
2. What is the signal Lady Macbeth is to give Macbeth to let him know that she has taken care of the guards (grooms)?
3. What excuse does Lady Macbeth give for not killing Duncan herself?
4. After Macbeth kills Duncan, he goes to Lady Macbeth and is concerned about not being able to say "Amen." What is her advice to him?
5. Then, Macbeth is worried about hearing a voice saying, "Macbeth does murder sleep." What does Lady Macbeth then tell him to do?
6. Why won't Macbeth take the daggers back to the scene of the crime?
7. Who was knocking?
8. What three things does drinking provoke?
9. How does Lennox describe the night, and what is Macbeth's response?
10. What did Macduff discover?
11. Macduff says, "Oh, gentle lady, 'Tis not for you to hear what I can speak. The repetition, in a woman's ear, Would murder as it fell." What is ironic about this?
12. What excuse or explanation did Macbeth give for killing the guards (grooms)? What is his real reason?
13. Why do Malcolm and Donalbain leave?
14. Why does Ross not believe Malcolm and Donalbain were responsible for Duncan's murder?

Macbeth Short Answer Study Questions Page 2

Act III
1. Why does Macbeth want Banquo and Fleance dead?
2. What is Macbeth's plan for killing Banquo and Fleance? Does it work?
3. Macbeth says, "The worm that's fled Hath nature that in time will venom breed, No teeth for the present." What does that mean?
4. Who (what) did Macbeth see at the banquet table?
5. How does Lady Macbeth cover for Macbeth at the banquet? What excuses does she give for his wild talk?
6. Who else was missing from the banquet table (besides Banquo)?
7. Macbeth says, "I am in blood Stepped in so far that should I wade no more, Returning were as tedious as go o'er." What does he mean?
8. What does Hecate want the witches to do?
9. What does Lennox think about Macbeth, Fleance, and Duncan's sons?

Act IV
1. Witch 2 says, "By the pricking of my thumb, Something wicked this way comes." Who comes?
2. What is Macbeth's attitude towards the witches this time?
3. What four things did the witches show Macbeth? What does each show/say? What is Macbeth's reaction?
4. Macbeth says (about the witches), "Infected be the air whereon they ride, And damned all those that trust them!" What is Macbeth, in effect, saying about himself?
5. Where is Macduff?
6. Why does Macbeth have Macduff's family and servants killed?
7. Why does Lady Macduff's son say liars and swearers are fools?
8. Malcolm says, "Angels are bright still, though the brightest fell. Though all things foul would wear the brows of grace, Yet grace must still look so." What does that mean?
9. Macduff says, "Oh, Scotland, Scotland!" Why?
10. What news does Ross bring to Macduff?

Act V
1. What do the doctor and gentlewoman see Lady Macbeth doing? What do they decide to do about it?
2. What does Macbeth want the doctor to do for his wife?
3. What trick does Malcolm use to hide the number of men in his army?
4. Malcolm says, "And none serve with him but constrained things Whose hearts are absent, too." What does that mean?
5. What is Macbeth's reaction to Lady Macbeth's death?
6. What is Macbeth's reaction to the news that Birnam Wood is moving?

Macbeth Short Answer Study Questions Page 3

7. Who first fights Macbeth? What happens?
8. Macbeth says to Macduff, "But get thee back, my soul is too much charged With blood of thine already." To what is he referring?
9. When does Macbeth know he's in trouble?
10. How does Macbeth die?
11. Who will be King of Scotland?

STUDY GUIDE QUESTIONS - *Macbeth*
Short Answer Format Answer Key

Act One

1. What is the point of the first scene literally and in reference to the whole play?
    Literally, the witches are deciding when they shall meet again. This scene sets the mood for the entire play, and introduces several major motifs: the witches (supernatural influences in the play), the idea of fair being foul, and the stormy fate of Scotland. The main character, Macbeth, is also introduced by name.

2. What does Duncan call Macbeth when he hears Macbeth has defeated Macdonwald?
    He calls him "valiant Cousin! Worthy gentleman!" This is ironic, being said to the man who will be his murderer.

3. Who is sentenced to death?
    The Thane of Cawdor is sentenced to death.

4. What do the witches predict in I.iii for Macbeth? For Banquo?
    They predict Macbeth will be Thane of Cawdor and eventually the king. They predict that Banquo will be "lesser than Macbeth, and greater, Not so happy, and yet happier" and that his descendants will be kings although he will not be one.

5. What news does Ross bring Macbeth?
    Ross tells Macbeth that Macbeth now holds the title of the Thane of Cawdor.

6. Banquo, like Macbeth, is surprised that the witches have predicted Macbeth's new title. He is, however, leery. What does he say about the motives of the "instruments of darkness"?
    He says they often tell of good things which may happen without telling the bad consequences.

7. Malcolm describes Cawdor's last moments before execution. What is Duncan's reply?
    You can't tell what is in a person's heart by looking at his face.

8. Macbeth says, "Stars, hide your fires, Let not light see my black and deep desires." What are Macbeth's desires?
    He now desires to be the king, and he realizes that something will have to be done with the present king (and his sons) before his desires can become reality.

9. After Lady Macbeth reads the letter, what does she tell us is her opinion of Macbeth, and how does she plan to help him?
    In short, Lady Macbeth thinks Macbeth could be a good king, but he lacks the hard-heartedness which would allow him to get to the position. She'll talk him into it.

10. What is Lady Macbeth's "prayer" to the spirits after she learns Duncan is coming"?
    She wants to be filled with cruelty, given a hard heart and the thick blood necessary to do what has to be done in order to make Macbeth king.

11. What advice does Lady Macbeth give Macbeth when he arrives home?
    She tells him he must learn to look innocent even when his heart is full of evil. He has to learn to hide his true feelings.

12. What are Macbeth's arguments to himself against killing Duncan?
    Macbeth is Duncan's kinsman and his subject. Duncan is a good king and virtuous man; he has done no particular evil. Duncan is a popular king, and his death would bring sorrow and unrest upon Scotland.

13. What arguments does Lady Macbeth use to convince Macbeth to commit the murder?
    She tells him not to be a coward, not to say later that he "could have been" when he could "be" king. She tells him to be a man and go get what he wants. She says if she had made the promise to do this, that she would have killed her own baby to carry forth with her promise.

14. What is Lady Macbeth's plan?
    She will drug the kings grooms (guards). Macbeth will then go into the king's room and murder him in his sleep.

Act II
1. What is Macbeth's lie to Banquo about the witches' predictions?
   He says he doesn't even think about them.

2. What is the signal Lady Macbeth is to give Macbeth to let him know that she has taken care of the guards (grooms)?
   She will ring a bell.

3. What excuse does Lady Macbeth give for not killing Duncan herself?
   He looked like her father sleeping there.

4. After Macbeth kills Duncan, he goes to Lady Macbeth and is concerned about not being able to say "Amen." What is her advice to him?
   She tells him not to think about it so much, or it will make them crazy. (Notice that she does later, in fact, go mad and commit suicide.)

5. Then, Macbeth is worried about hearing a voice saying, "Macbeth does murder sleep." What does Lady Macbeth then tell him to do?
   She tells him to go get some water and wash "this filthy witness" from his hands. In other words, get cleaned up and forget about it.

6. Why won't Macbeth take the daggers back to the scene of the crime?
   He can't bear to look at Duncan again.

7. Who was knocking?
   Macduff and Lennox were knocking at the gate.

8. What three things does drinking provoke?
   It provokes "nose-painting, sleep, and urine."

9. How does Lennox describe the night, and what is Macbeth's response?
   Lennox goes through a great description of the terrible night, saying it predicted terrible, confusing times ahead. Macbeth brushes it off by saying it was a "rough night."

10. What did Macduff discover?
    Macduff discovered Duncan's body.

11. Macduff says, "Oh, gentle lady, 'Tis not for you to hear what I can speak. The repetition, in a woman's ear, Would murder as it fell." What is ironic about this?
    Lady Macbeth was a determining force in the death of Duncan. She is no "lady."

12. What excuse or explanation did Macbeth give for killing the guards (grooms)? What is his real reason?
    He did it out of pain and rage, but he actually wanted to be rid of any possible witnesses to the murder.

13. Why do Malcolm and Donalbain leave?
    They fear that the king's murderer will be after them, too.

14. Why does Ross not believe Malcolm and Donalbain were responsible for Duncan's murder?
    He says it is against nature -- both their personal natures and nature as the ruling force in the universe.

Act III
1. Why does Macbeth want Banquo and Fleance dead?
   He knows they suspect him of foul play, and he is furious that he has done all of the work (so-to-speak) of becoming king, and Banquo's descendants will benefit from it.

2. What is Macbeth's plan for killing Banquo and Fleance? Does it work?
   He gets two convicted murderers to wait along the road to ambush them. The murderers kill Banquo, but Fleance escapes.

3. Macbeth says, "The worm that's fled Hath nature that in time will venom breed, No teeth for the present." What does that mean?

   Fleance will be a problem in the future, since he will have children who will become kings, but for now Macbeth can let him go and deal with other things because Fleance is of no immediate threat to him personally.

4. Who (what) did Macbeth see at the banquet table?

   He saw Banquo's ghost.

5. How does Lady Macbeth cover for Macbeth at the banquet? What excuses does she give for his wild talk?

   She tells the guests that he often has these fits, that those who know him well have learned to ignore them. When Macbeth really gets out of hand, she sends the guests home.

6. Who else was missing from the banquet table (besides Banquo)?

   Macduff is missing.

7. Macbeth says, "I am in blood Stepped in so far that should I wade no more, Returning were as tedious as go o'er." What does he mean?

   There is no going back now. Macbeth is committed to this course of action, whatever terrible things he may yet have to do.

8. What does Hecate want the witches to do?

   She wants the witches to give Macbeth some visions which will give him false impressions, false hopes for his personal safety and the safety of his rule, so he will continue on his path of destruction.

9. What does Lennox think about Macbeth, Fleance, and Duncan's sons?

   He thinks Macbeth is the "good guy," Fleance killed Banquo, and Duncan's sons killed the king.

Act IV

1. Witch 2 says, "By the pricking of my thumb, Something wicked this way comes." Who comes?

   Macbeth comes.

2. What is Macbeth's attitude towards the witches this time?

   He is demanding, trying to take charge.

3. What four things did the witches show Macbeth? What does each show/say? What is Macbeth's reaction?
    They showed him an armed head, a bloody child, a crowned child with a tree in its hand, and, finally, eight kings followed by Banquo's ghost. Respectively, they showed/told Macbeth to beware of Macduff, that he would not be harmed by anyone "born of woman," that he would not be vanquished until Birnam Wood would come to Dunsinane, and that Banquo's descendants would be kings.

4. Macbeth says (about the witches), "Infected be the air whereon they ride, And damned all those that trust them!" What is Macbeth, in effect, saying about himself?
    He is damned.

5. Where is Macduff?
    He is in England helping Malcolm.

6. Why does Macbeth have Macduff's family and servants killed?
    Macduff is not loyal to Macbeth, and Macbeth is angry.

7. Why does Lady Macduff's son say liars and swearers are fools?
    He implies that since there are more of them than honest people, they should get together and hang the honest folks. They are foolish to leave themselves in jeopardy when they could overcome the honest people.

8. Malcolm says, "Angels are bright still, though the brightest fell. Though all things foul would wear the brows of grace, Yet grace must still look so." What does that mean?
    The devil was, of course, at one time the brightest angel. The point is that things aren't what they seem. One can't judge the book by its cover, so-to-speak.

9. Macduff says, "Oh, Scotland, Scotland!" Why?
    Malcolm has just told him what a horrid king he (Malcolm) would be if he were on the throne instead of Macbeth. Given a choice, then, between Malcolm and Macbeth, he gravely fears for his country's future.

10. What news does Ross bring to Macduff?
    Ross brings news of Macduff's family's murders.

Act V

1. What do the doctor and gentlewoman see Lady Macbeth doing? What do they decide to do?
    She is sleepwalking and talking about the murders. The doctor decides his best move is to not mention that he heard anything, and he tells the woman to keep an eye on Lady Macbeth.

2. What does Macbeth want the doctor to do for his wife?
    He wants the doctor to ease her suffering, to give her something to make her oblivious to her weighty troubles.

3. What trick does Malcolm use to hide the number of men in his army?
    He has his men cut off tree branches and use them as camouflage.

4. Malcolm says, "And none serve with him but constrained things Whose hearts are absent, too." What does that mean?
    Macbeth's armies are there in body only, not in spirit, and there should not be any serious opposition.

5. What is Macbeth's reaction to Lady Macbeth's death?
    He takes it very calmly, saying she would have died sooner or later, anyway.

6. What is Macbeth's reaction to the news that Birnam Wood is moving?
    "Arm, arm, and out!" He's going to fight to the bitter end and take down the whole universe with him, if necessary.

7. Who first fights Macbeth? What happens?
    Young Siward fights Macbeth and is slain.

8. Macbeth says to Macduff, "But get thee back, my soul is too much charged With blood of thine already." To what is he referring?
    Macbeth doesn't want to fight Macduff; he has already killed Macduff's family.

9. When does Macbeth know he's in trouble?
    He knows this is his end when Macduff tells him he was taken from his mother's womb instead of being "born of woman."

10. How does Macbeth die?
    Macduff fights him and beheads him.

11. Who will be King of Scotland?
    Malcolm will be king.

MULTIPLE CHOICE STUDY GUIDE/QUIZ QUESTIONS - *Macbeth*

Act One

1. Which motif is not introduced in the first scene?
    a. Supernatural influences
    b. Man as a sinner
    c. Fair being foul
    d. The stormy fate of Scotland

2. What does Duncan call Macbeth when he hears Macbeth has defeated Macdonwald?
    a. "Treacherous rebel! Despised rogue!"
    b. "Your Majesty, Lord of all Scotland!"
    c. "Murderous beast! Evil of soul!"
    d. "Valiant Cousin! Worthy gentleman!"

3. Who is sentenced to death?
    a. Duncan
    b. Ross
    c. The Thane of Cawdor
    d. The Captain

4. What do the witches predict in I.iii for Macbeth? For Banquo?
    a. Macbeth will be Thane of Cawdor and eventually the king. Banquo's descendants will be king, although he will not.
    b. Macbeth will be conqueror of Norway, Banquo will be king.
    c. Macbeth will remain Thane of Glamis. Banquo will be Thane of Cawdor, neither will ever be king.
    d. Macbeth will be king. Banquo will be Thane of Glamis and Cawdor.

5. What news does Ross bring Macbeth?
    a. Lady Macbeth has had a son
    b. The Thane of Glamis has been killed
    c. Macbeth now holds the title of the Thane of Cawdor
    d. The army has just lost the battle with the Norwegians.

6. What does Banquo say about the motives of the "instruments of darkness?"
    a. They often tell of good things without telling the bad consequences.
    b. They are greedy and only make predictions when someone pays enough.
    c. Good conquers evil, and their predictions will not come true.
    d. The witches are crazy, and don't know what they are saying.

Study Guide/Quiz Questions - *Macbeth* - Multiple Choice Format - Page 2

7. Malcom describes Cawdor's last moments before execution. What is Duncan's reply?
    a. You should never turn your back, even on a friend.
    b. You shouldn't sympathize for one who has committed evil deeds.
    c. You should always be ready for you never know when death will strike
    d. You can't tell what is in a person's heart by looking at his face.

8. Macbeth says, "Stars, hide your fires, Let not light see my black and deep desires." What are Macbeth's desires?
    a. He wants to go home to see Lady Macbeth
    b. He wants to raise the taxes in the lands he rules
    c. He is very tired. He wants the stars to stop shining so he can sleep.
    d. He wants to be king

9. After Lady Macbeth reads the letter, what does she tell us is her opinion of Macbeth, and how does she plan to help him?
    a. She doesn't think he would be a good king, but since he is her husband, she will support him in whatever he wants to do.
    b. She thinks he could be a good king, but he lacks the hard-heartedness which would allow him to get the position. She will talk him into it.
    c. She does not want him to be king, and vows to stop him.
    d She thinks Banquo would be a better king, she plans to convince Macbeth to support Banquo instead.

10. What is Lady Macbeth's "prayer" to the spirits after she learns Duncan is coming"?
    a. She wants to be filled with cruelty, given the hard heart and thick blood necessary to do what has to be done to make Macbeth king.
    b. She prays that Duncan will die on the way to see Macbeth. She asks the witches to create a terrible storm.
    c. She wants her husband's nerve to become stronger so that she will not have to do the actual stabbing.
    d. She asks for a sign that her decision is the right one for her husband and for the country.

11. What advice does Lady Macbeth give Macbeth when he arrives home?
    a. He should not eat too much, because he does not want to get too tired and sluggish, or he won't be able to commit the murder quickly.
    b. He should let Banquo in on the plan so that he has more help.
    c. He must learn to look innocent even when his heart is full of evil.
    d. This would not be a good time to murder Duncan. They should wait a few days.

Study Guide/Quiz Questions - *Macbeth* - Multiple Choice Format - Page 3

12. What are Macbeth's arguments to himself against killing Duncan?
    a. There are too many witnesses in the castle. He could never get away with it.
    b. Macbeth is Duncan's kinsman and subject. Duncan is a good and popular king; his death would bring sorrow to Scotland.
    c. Macbeth doesn't really have the ambition to be king. He is doing this to please his wife. He may be able to change her mind.
    d. If anyone found out he did it, they would just kill him. He is better off being a Thane and being alive.

13. What arguments does Lady Macbeth use to convince Macbeth to commit the murder?
    a. She tells him not be to a coward, but to be a man and go and get what he wants.
    b. She tells him that if Duncan suspects anything and they aren't successful they will lose their lives, so he should go ahead with the plan
    c. She says that the people of Scotland will grow to love Macbeth even more than they love Duncan. He should go ahead for the good of the country.
    d. She reminds him that when they got married he promised to always make her happy, and she won't be happy until he is the king.

14. What is Lady Macbeth's plan?
    a. She will put poison in the king's food. He will die in his sleep and it will look like a natural death.
    b. They will bribe the guards and offer them money and power to kill the king.
    c. Macbeth's soldiers will come into the banquet disguised as robbers. They will commit the murder and wound Macbeth so that it doesn't look suspicious.
    d. She will drug the king's guards. Macbeth will then go into the king's room and kill him.

Study Guide/Quiz Questions - *Macbeth* - Multiple Choice Format - Page 4

Act II

15. What is Macbeth's lie to Banquo about the witches' predictions?
    a. He says he does not remember what they said.
    b. He says he does not even think about them.
    c. He says they made a lucky guess on their predictions, but they are wrong about him ever being king.
    d. He says only fools and women believe such nonsense.

16. What is the signal Lady Macbeth is to give Macbeth to let him know that she has taken care of the guards?
    a. She will ring a bell.
    b. She will send a servant to say she is ill and wants to see him.
    c. She will light three candles in her bedroom window.
    d. She will stand at the window and whistle like a bird.

17. What excuse does Lady Macbeth give for not killing Duncan herself?
    a. It would diminish Macbeth's power if she did the killing.
    b. She is not a strong and might not be able to use the knife effectively.
    c. She saw in a dream that only Macbeth could commit the murder.
    d. He reminded him of her father sleeping there.

18. After Macbeth kills Duncan, he goes to Lady Macbeth and is concerned about not being able to say "Amen." What is her advice to him?
    a. He should keep trying and soon he will succeed
    b. It does not matter whether or not he can say it
    c. They shouldn't think about it or it will make them crazy
    d. After things calm down he can go to the priest and ask for forgiveness

19. Then, Macbeth is worried about hearing a voice saying, "Macbeth does murder sleep." What does Lady Macbeth then tell him to do?
    a. Have a glass of wine and relax
    b. Get cleaned up and forget about it
    c. Have the minstrel come and sing some quiet tunes to put them to sleep
    d. Go for a walk in the garden and get some fresh air.

20. Why won't Macbeth take the daggers back to the scene of the crime?
    a. He can't bear to look at Duncan again
    b. He is afraid to be seen and look suspicious
    c. He thinks it will be bad luck to touch them again
    d. He says he has done enough; Lady Macbeth can return the daggers

Study Guide/Quiz Questions - *Macbeth* - Multiple Choice Format - Page 5

21. Who was knocking?
    a. The servant was bringing a glass of wine to Macbeth's chamber
    b. Macduff and Lennox were at the gate
    c. A drunkard who had lost his way home wanted a place to sleep
    d. A messenger came with a note for Lady Macbeth

22. What three things does drinking provoke?
    a. "Sin, ill tempers, and ruin"
    b. "Poor health, nightmares, and poverty"
    c. "Nose-painting, sleep and urine"
    d. "Fighting, hatred and trouble"

23. How does Lennox describe the night, and what is Macbeth's response?
    a. Lennox says it was a terrible night, and it predicted terrible, confusing times ahead. Macbeth brushes it off and says it was merely a rough night.
    b. Lennox says it was truly beautiful and peaceful-looking. Macbeth says appearances can be deceiving.
    c. Lennox says it was an awful night. Macbeth agrees and blames the witches.
    d. Lennox says it started out looking like an ordinary night. Macbeth disagrees and says it was terrible.

24. What did Macduff discover?
    a. A note containing the outline of a plot to kill Duncan.
    b. An unlocked gate and a drunk porter
    c. Another omen -- dead flowers in the garden
    d. Duncan's body

25. Macduff says, "Oh, gentle lady, 'Tis not for you to hear what I can speak. The repetition, in a woman's ear, Would murder as it fell." What is ironic about this?
    a. He pretended to be brave, but he really wasn't.
    b. He sounded concerned about Lady Macbeth, but he really thought women were weak and foolish
    c. He tried to sound upset, but he was glad the king was dead.
    d. He didn't know about Lady Macbeth's part in the murder

Study Guide/Quiz Questions - *Macbeth* - Multiple Choice Format - Page 6

26. What excuse did Macbeth give for killing the guards (grooms)? What is his real reason?
    a. He was drunk and didn't realize what he had done. He didn't want anyone to suspect Lady Macbeth.
    b. He did it out of pain and rage, but he actually wanted to be rid of any possible witnesses.
    c. They were attacking him, and he did it in self defense. He wanted it to look like a plot to murder him, too.
    d. The witches predicted it, and he could not help himself. He was afraid they would not be loyal to him once he became king.

27. Why do Malcom and Donalbain leave?
    a. They don't want to be accused of the crime.
    b. They are going to take the sad news to their mother.
    c. They are afraid the murderer will be after them, too.
    d. They want to start making the funeral arrangements.

28. Why does Ross not believe Malcom and Donalbain were responsible for Duncan's murder?
    a. He was with them and knows they are innocent.
    b. It was against their personal natures and against nature as the ruling force in the universe.
    c. They know that killing their father would only provoke a fight between themselves, and one or both of them would probably be killed.
    d. Both are too weak, cowardly, and unambitious to want to be king.

Study Guide/Quiz Questions - *Macbeth* - Multiple Choice Format - Page 7

Act III

29. Why does Macbeth want Banquo and Fleance dead?
    a. He knows they suspect him. He is furious that he has done the work to become king, and Banquo's descendants will benefit
    b. He thinks they suspect him, and that they may try to kill Lady Macbeth in retaliation.
    c. He is afraid they will try to bring Malcom and Donalbain back and make one of them king instead
    d. He has gone crazy and wants to kill anyone associated with Duncan

30. What is Macbeth's plan for killing Banquo and Fleance? Does it work?
    a. He poisons their meal and they both die
    b. He has his soldiers attack them, Banquo is wounded but Fleance dies
    c. He plans to kill them that night. They find out and both escape
    d. He gets two convicted murderers to wait along the road and ambush them. Banquo is killed but Fleance escapes.

31. Macbeth says, "The worm that's fled Hath nature that in time will venom breed, No teeth for the present." What does that mean?
    a. He is having nightmares about snakes.
    b. Once a man commits murder he has the urge to do it again.
    c. Fleance's descendants will be a problem in the future, but Fleance is no immediate threat, so Macbeth will not pursue him now
    d. He regrets that he and lady Macbeth have no children to carry on his reign after he dies.

32. Who (what) did Macbeth see at the banquet table?
    a. The three witches laughing at him
    b. Banquo's ghost
    c. Blood from the daggers in his wine cup
    d. The image of Duncan's beating heart

33. How does Lady Macbeth cover for Macbeth at the banquet?
    a. She tells the guests he often has fits. When he really gets out of hand she sends the guests home.
    b. She pretends to be ill and convinces him to go to their chambers. She asks Macduff to entertain the guests.
    c. She says he is still grieving for Duncan. She gives him wine to quiet him, and she hosts the banquet.
    d. She laughs and says he is in high spirits. She encourages the others to make merry with her and Macbeth.

Study Guide/Quiz Questions - *Macbeth* - Multiple Choice Format - Page 8

34. Who else was missing from the banquet table besides Banquo?
    a. Lady Macbeth
    b. Macbeth
    c. Macduff
    d. Lennox

35. Macbeth says, "I am in blood Stepped in so far that should I wade no more, Returning were as tedious as go o'er." What does he mean?
    a. He is sorry for what he did and will give up the throne
    b. He is committed to his course of action whatever he has to do.
    c. He is still alive and intends to stay that way
    d. He does not want to return to see the room where he killed Duncan

36. What does Hecate want the witches to do?
    a. Put a spell on Macbeth to make him invincible
    b. Leave the country before Macbeth bothers them again.
    c. Give Macbeth some visions to give him false hopes for his safety so he will continue on his path of construction.
    d. Haunt Macbeth's dreams so that he realizes the evil thing he has done.

37. What does Lennox think about Macbeth, Fleance, and Duncan's sons?
    a. They are all in on the plot together
    b. Macbeth is a murderer, the others are innocent
    c. Macbeth is innocent, Fleance killed Banquo, and Banquo killed Duncan
    d. Macbeth is good, Fleance killed Banquo and Duncan's son killed him

Study Guide/Quiz Questions - *Macbeth* - Multiple Choice Format - Page 9

Act IV

38. Witch 2 says, "By the pricking of my thumb, Something wicked this way comes." Who comes?
    a. Banquo's ghost
    b. Macbeth
    c. Donalbain
    d. Hecate

39. What is Macbeth's attitude towards the witches this time?
    a. He is demanding, trying to take charge
    b. He is scared and full of remorse
    c. He is kind and considerate, trying to get them to help him
    d. He is rude, saying he has no further need of them

40. Match the four things the witches showed and what each one shows.
    ___ 1. an armed head
    ___ 2. a bloodied child
    ___ 3. a crowned child with a tree in its hand
    ___ 4. eight kings followed by banquo's ghost

    a. Banquo's descendants would be kings
    b. Macbeth should beware of Macduff
    c. He would not be vanquished until Birnam Wood would come to Dunsinane
    d. He would not be harmed by anyone "born of woman."

41. Macbeth says (about the witches), "Infected be the air whereon they ride, And damned all those that trust them!" What is he saying about himself?
    a. He is damned
    b. He has been poisoned by them
    c. He is too trusting a person
    d. He is stronger than they are

42. Where is Macduff?
    a. He is keeping vigil over Duncan's grave
    b. He has fled to France
    c. He is in England helping Malcom
    d. He has barricaded himself in his room at the castle

Study Guide/Quiz Questions - *Macbeth* - Multiple Choice Format - Page 10

43. Why does Macbeth have Macduff's family and servants killed?
    a. Macbeth is angry because Macduff has not been loyal to him.
    b. The witches told him to do it.
    c. Lady Macbeth does not get along with them
    d. He wants to lure Macduff back from England

44. Why does Lady Macduff's son say liars and swearers are fools?
    a. They are foolish to think they can get away with their dishonesty
    b. They should not leave themselves in jeopardy when they could overcome and hang the honest people
    c. People who have any intelligence don't lie and swear
    d. They don't realize the rewards of a virtuous life

45. Malcom says, "Angels are bright still, though the brightest fell. Though all things foul would wear the brows of grace, Yet grace must still look so." What does that mean?
    a. It is almost dawn. Thing will look brighter in the morning.
    b. God forgives all who repent
    c. Things are not always what they seem
    d. Even good men sometimes make mistakes.

46. Why does Macduff says, "Oh, Scotland, Scotland?"
    a. He misses his family
    b. He fears for his country's future
    c. It is a curse against Macbeth
    d. It is a promise to be loyal to his country

47. What news does Ross bring to Macduff?
    a. The army is ready to march against Macbeth
    b. Duncan's sons have been found
    c. It is safe for Macduff to return home
    d. Lady Macduff and the children have been murdered

Study Guide/Quiz Questions - *Macbeth* - Multiple Choice Format - Page 11

Act V

48. What do the doctor and gentlewoman see Lady Macbeth doing? What do they decide to do about it?
    a. She is sleepwalking and talking about the murders. They decide to keep an eye on her, but not say anything.
    b. She is crying and tearing at her clothes. The doctor gives her something to make her sleep and tells the gentlewoman to stay close by.
    c. She is sleepwalking and calling out to Macbeth. The doctor wakes her up and then locks her in her room, with the gentlewoman on guard.
    d. She is singing and dancing. They think she is fine and they accompany her.

49. What does Macbeth want the doctor to do for his wife?
    a. Take her to his house in the country for a rest
    b. Listen to her talk about her problems
    c. Take her to priest for confession
    d. Give her something to make her unaware of her troubles

50. What trick does Malcom use to hide the number of men in his army?
    a. He has them march very closely next to each other
    b. He only brings half of them forward at first
    c. He has them use tree branches as camouflage
    d. He marches at night so the enemy can't see to count them

51. Malcom says, "And none serve with him but constrained things Whose hearts are absent, too." What does that mean?
    a. Macbeth is being haunted by the ghosts of Duncan and Banquo
    b. Macbeth's armies are there in body but not spirit, and should be easy to defeat
    c. The witches played an evil trick on Macbeth and deserve punishment
    d. He is mourning for all of the soldiers who will die in the battle

52. What is Macbeth's reaction to Lady Macbeth's death?
    a. He is glad, because now his secret has died with her
    b. He is calm, saying she would have died sooner or later, anyway
    c. He flies into a rage and kills the doctor
    d. He calls on the witches to bring her back to life

53. What is Macbeth's reaction to the news that Birnam Wood is moving?
    a. He laughs and says it is an illusion
    b. He is afraid and barricades himself in the castle
    c. He vows to fight to the bitter end
    d. He order his men to set fire to the woods

Study Guide/Quiz Questions - *Macbeth* - Multiple Choice Format - Page 12

54. Who first fights Macbeth? What happens?
    a. Seyton, and he wounds Macbeth
    b. Malcom and they are both wounded
    c. Ross, and he defeats Macbeth
    d. Young Siward, and he is killed

55. Macbeth says to Macduff, "But get thee back, my soul is too much charged With blood of thine already." To what is he referring?
    a. Macbeth doesn't want to fight Macduff; he has already killed Macduff's family
    b. Macbeth has the urge to kill anyone who comes near him
    c. Macbeth is wounded and wants compassion
    d. Macbeth is ready to stop the bloodshed and give up the throne

56. When does Macbeth know he's in trouble?
    a. He sees the actual size of the army
    b. Macduff tells him he was taken from his mother's womb instead of being "born of woman."
    c. He sees his wife's ghost in front of him
    d. He feels dizzy and he is not able to pick up his sword

57. How does Macbeth die?
    a. Macduff beheads him
    b. He accidentally falls on his own sword
    c. One of his own soldiers mistakenly kills him
    d. He is attacked by a group of Macduff's soldiers

58. Who will be King of Scotland?
    a. Ross
    b. Macduff
    c. Malcom
    d. Siward

ANSWER KEY - MULTIPLE CHOICE STUDY/QUIZ QUESTIONS
Macbeth

Act I	Act II	Act III	Act IV	Act V
1. B	15. B	29. A	38. B	48. A
2. D	16. A	30. D	39. A	49. D
3. C	17. D	31. C	40. 1=B, 2=D, 3=C, 4=A	50. C
4. A	18. C	32. B	41. A	51. B
5. C	19. B	33. A	42. C	52. B
6. A	20. A	34. C	43. A	53. C
7. D	21. B	35. B	44. B	54. D
8. D	22. C	36. C	45. C	55. A
9. B	23. A	37. D	46. B	56. B
10. A	24. D		47. D	57. A
11. C	25. D			58. C
12. B	26. B			
13. A	27. C			
14. D	28. B			

PREREADING VOCABULARY WORKSHEETS

VOCABULARY - *Macbeth*

Act I

Part I: Using Prior Knowledge and Contextual Clues

Below are the sentences in which the vocabulary words appear in the text. Read the sentence. Use any clues you can find in the sentence combined with your prior knowledge, and write what you think the underlined words mean on the lines provided.

1. Like valor's minion carved out his passage

___

2. Into the air, and what seemed corporal melted

___

3. Like our strange garments, cleave not to their mold

___

4. I'll be myself the harbinger and make joyful the hearing of my wife with your approach

___

5. And chastise with the valor of my tongue

___

6. To beguile the time, look like the time, bear welcome in your eye

___

7. Upon the sightless couriers of the air

___

Macbeth Vocabulary Act I Continued

Part II: Determining the Meaning

You have tried to figure out the meanings of the vocabulary words for <u>Act I</u>. Now match the vocabulary words to their dictionary definitions. If there are words for which you cannot figure out the definition by contextual clues and by process of elimination, look them up in a dictionary.

___ 1. minion   A. of or relating to the body
___ 2. corporal   B. one that indicates or foreshadows what is to come
___ 3. cleave   C. to punish
___ 4. harbinger   D. to pass time pleasantly
___ 5. chastise   E. messengers
___ 6. beguile   F. to adhere, cling, or stick fast
___ 7. couriers   G. an obsequious follower or dependent

Vocabulary - Macbeth Act II

Part I: Using Prior Knowledge and Contextual Clues
Below are the sentences in which the vocabulary words appear in the text. Read the sentence. Use any clues you can find in the sentence combined with your prior knowledge, and write what you think the underlined words mean on the lines provided.

8. I see thee yet, in form as palpable

_____

9. How is't with me when every noise appalls me?

_____

10. Faith, sir, we were carousing till the second cock.

_____

11. ...equivocates him in a sleep and giving him the lie, leaves him.

_____

12. Fears and scruples shake us.

_____

13. What good could they pretend? They were suborned.

_____

Part II: Determining the Meaning
You have tried to figure out the meanings of the vocabulary words for Act II. Now match the vocabulary words to their dictionary definitions. If there are words for which you cannot figure out the definition by contextual clues and by process of elimination, look them up in a dictionary.

___ 8. palpable   A. Fills with dismay
___ 9. appalls   B. Avoids making an explicit statement
___ 10. carousing   C. Conscience; morals
___ 11. equivocates   D. Easily perceived
___ 12. scruples   E. Induced to commit an unlawful act
___ 13. suborned   F. Drunken merrymaking

Vocabulary - *Macbeth* Act III

Part I: Using Prior Knowledge and Contextual Clues

Below are the sentences in which the vocabulary words appear in the text. Read the sentence. Use any clues you can find in the sentence combined with your prior knowledge, and write what you think the underlined words mean on the lines provided.

14. Their cruel parricide, filling their hearers with strange invention.

_____

15. She'll close and be herself, whilst our poor malice Remains in danger

_____

16. And make our faces vizards to our hearts.

_____

17. Aye, my good lord. Safe in a ditch he bides, with twenty trenched gashes on his head.

_____

18. Ere humane statute purged the gentle weal -

_____

19. Do not muse at me, my most worthy friends.

_____

20. Do faithful homage and receive free honors.

_____

Macbeth Vocabulary Act III Continued

Part II: Determining the Meaning
   You have tried to figure out the meanings of the vocabulary words for Act III. Now match the vocabulary words to their dictionary definitions. If there are words for which you cannot figure out the definition by contextual clues and by process of elimination, look them up in a dictionary.

___ 14. parricide   A. special honor expressed publicly
___ 15. malice   B. freed from impurities
___ 16. vizards   C. to consider
___ 17. bides   D. the murdering of one's parent(s)
___ 18. purged   E. masks
___ 19. muse   F. waits
___ 20. homage   G. extreme ill-will or spite

Vocabulary - *Macbeth* Act IV

Part I: Using Prior Knowledge and Contextual Clues
  Below are the sentences in which the vocabulary words appear in the text. Read the sentence. Use any clues you can find in the sentence combined with your prior knowledge, and write what you think the underlined words mean on the lines provided.

21. Double, double toil and trouble, Fire burn and cauldron bubble.

_____

22. Let this pernicious hour stand aye accursed in the calendar!

_____

23. The most diminutive of birds, will fight, her young ones in her nest, against the owl.

_____

24. You may deserve of him through me, and wisdom to offer up a weak, poor, innocent lamb to appease an angry god.

_____

25. I grant him bloody, luxurious, avaricious false, deceitful, sudden, malicious, smaking of every sin that has a name.

_____

26. By his own interdiction stands accursed, and does blaspheme his breed?

_____

27. Child of integrity, hath from my soul wiped the black scruples, reconciled my thoughts to thy good truth and honor.

_____

Macbeth Vocabulary Act IV Continued

Part II: Determining the Meaning

You have tried to figure out the meanings of the vocabulary words for Act IV. Now match the vocabulary words to their dictionary definitions. If there are words for which you cannot figure out the definition by contextual clues and by process of elimination, look them up in a dictionary.

___ 21. caldron   A. evil; wicked
___ 22. pernicious   B. to humor; make peace with
___ 23. diminutive   C. something authoritatively forbidden
___ 24. appease   D. a large vessel
___ 25. avaricious   E. adherence to a strict moral code
___ 26. interdiction   F. extremely small in size
___ 27. integrity   G. having an immoderate desire for wealth

Vocabulary - *Macbeth* Act V

Part I: Using Prior Knowledge and Contextual Clues
    Below are the sentences in which the vocabulary words appear in the text. Read the sentence. Use any clues you can find in the sentence combined with your prior knowledge, and write what you think the underlined words mean on the lines provided.

28. Let our just <u>censures</u> attend the true event, and put we on industrious soldiership.

_____

29. Till famine and the <u>ague</u> eat them up.

_____

30. But swords I smile at, weapons laugh to scorn, <u>brandished</u> by man that's of a woman born.

_____

Part II: Determining the Meaning
    You have tried to figure out the meanings of the vocabulary words for Act V. Now match the vocabulary words to their dictionary definitions. If there are words for which you cannot figure out the definition by contextual clues and by process of elimination, look them up in a dictionary.

___ 28. censures   A. waved or flourished
___ 29. ague   B. harsh criticisms
___ 30. brandished   C. a chill or fit of shivering

ANSWER KEY - VOCABULARY
Macbeth

Act I	Act II	Act III	Act IV	Act V
1. G	8. D	14. D	21. D	28. B
2. A	9. A	15. G	22. A	29. C
3. F	10. F	16. E	23. F	30. A
4. B	11. B	17. F	24. B	
5. C	12. C	18. B	25. G	
6. D	13. E	19. C	26. C	
7. E		20. A	27. E	

DAILY LESSONS

LESSON ONE

Objectives
1. To gather background information
2. To give students the opportunity to fulfill their nonfiction reading assignment
3. To give students practice using the resources in the library
4. To distribute the materials which will be used in the unit

Activity #1

Distribute the materials which will be used in this unit. Explain in detail how students are to use these materials.

Study Guides Students should read the study guide questions for each reading assignment prior to beginning the reading assignment to get a feeling for what events and ideas are important in the section they are about to read. After reading the section, students will (as a class or individually) answer the questions to review the important events and ideas from that section of the play. Students should keep the study guides as study materials for the unit test.

Vocabulary Prior to reading a reading assignment, students will do vocabulary work related to the section of the play they are about to read. Following the completion of the reading of the play, there will be a vocabulary review of all the words used in the vocabulary assignments. Students should keep their vocabulary work as study materials for the unit test.

Reading Assignment Sheet You need to fill in the reading assignment sheet to let students know by when their reading has to be completed. You can either write the assignment sheet up on a side blackboard or bulletin board and leave it there for students to see each day, or you can "ditto" copies for each student to have. In either case, you should advise students to become very familiar with the reading assignments so they know what is expected of them.

Extra Activities Center The Extra Activities portion of this unit contains suggestions for an extra library of related plays and articles in your classroom as well as crossword and word search puzzles. Make an extra activities center in your room where you will keep these materials for students to use. (Bring the books and articles in from the library and keep several copies of the puzzles on hand.) Explain to students that these materials are available for students to use when they finish reading assignments or other class work early.

<u>Nonfiction Assignment Sheet</u> Explain to students that they each are to read at least one non-fiction piece from the in-class library at some time during the unit. Students will fill out a nonfiction assignment sheet after completing the reading to help you evaluate their reading experiences and to help the students think about and evaluate their own reading experiences.

<u>Books</u> Each school has its own rules and regulations regarding student use of school books. Advise students of the procedures that are normal for your school.

<u>Activity #2</u>
Take students to your school library. Distribute the Research Assignment Sheet. Discuss the directions in detail, and give students ample time to complete the assignment. Depending on how quickly your students work, you may also need to spend part of the class period for Lesson Two in the library.

RESEARCH ASSIGNMENT - *Macbeth*

Purposes
1. To give you some background information about Shakespeare, *Macbeth* and the historical era in which the play was written and performed
2. To help you fulfill the nonfiction reading assignment which is a part of this unit

Assignment

Use the resources of your library and/or media center to find out as much as you can about the topic your group has been assigned. Take notes so you remember what you have read, seen or heard. After you have collected your information, get together with the other members of your group to compile a "Fact Sheet," an outline of the facts you have gathered. You will be asked to give an oral report to share your information with the rest of your classmates so that everyone in your class will have information about each of the topics assigned. The "Fact Sheet" you prepare will be the basis of your oral report and, if duplicated, will serve as a study guide for you and your classmates.

If you wish, you may use this assignment to fulfill your nonfiction reading assignment for this unit. If you choose to do so, be sure to fill out your Nonfiction Reading Assignment Sheet.

Group 1: Research Shakespeare. Pretend as if you had to write a book about Shakespeare (a biography). Include information about his personal life, professional life, important events and influences in his life, and any topics of controversy surrounding his life.

Group 2: Research British History 1550-1650. What was going on in Britain during the time just before, during and just after Shakespeare lived? Who were the rulers? What was the political atmosphere? What were the people concerned about? How did the people live? Answer these kinds of questions in your report.

Group 3: Research World History 1550-1650. What was going on in the rest of the world (besides Britain) during this period?

Group 4: Research *Macbeth*. What is the play about? Why is it famous? What do critics say about it? Has there been more than one version of the play? Which one(s) are most often performed? Why? Which is/was the best production of the play? What difficulties are there in performing the play (if any)?

Getting Started

There are many sources of information for your research. Books, periodicals (magazines & journals), films/filmstrips/videos, and encyclopedias are some of the most commonly used research materials. Each member of your group should use a different source of materials. For example, one member should look for books, another should look for articles in periodicals, etc.

NONFICTION ASSIGNMENT SHEET
(To be completed after reading the required nonfiction article)

Name _____ Date _____

Title of Nonfiction Read _____

Written By _____ Publication Date _____

I. Factual Summary: Write a short summary of the piece you read.

II. Vocabulary
    1. With which vocabulary words in the piece did you encounter some degree of difficulty?

    2. How did you resolve your lack of understanding with these words?

III. Interpretation: What was the main point the author wanted you to get from reading his work?

IV. Criticism
    1. With which points of the piece did you agree or find easy to accept? Why?

    2. With which points of the piece did you disagree or find difficult to believe? Why?

V. Personal Response: What do you think about this piece? <u>OR</u> How does this piece influence your ideas?

LESSON TWO

Objectives
    1. To give students time to finish their research
    2. To give students time to compile their fact sheets
    3. To evaluate students' research
    4. To have students share all the information they have found

Activity #1
    Give students ample time to complete their research and compile their research fact sheets.

Activity #2
    Have one student from each group give an oral report to the class summarizing the information all the group members found. If you choose, students could just listen instead of taking notes, and you could duplicate the fact sheets for distribution in the next class period. The other alternative is to have students take notes from the class reports so they have study materials.

LESSON THREE

Objectives
1. To assign reading parts for Act I
2. To do the prereading activities for Act I

Activity #1

Explain that because *Macbeth* is a play it is meant to be acted on a stage. If you are not planning a production of the play, explain to students that the next best thing we can do is to read the parts orally. Each person in class will (eventually) have a speaking part to perform. The part does not have to be memorized, but the students' oral reading will be evaluated.

Make the reading part assignments for Act I, which will be read in Lesson Five. (Tell students the day and date that their reading will be done.)

Narrator (stage descriptions and directions; italicized)
Witch 1	Witch 2
Witch 3	Lennox
Malcolm	Duncan
Sergeant	Angus
Ross	Banquo
Macbeth	Lady Macbeth
Messenger	

Activity #3

Prior to reading Act I, students should preview the study questions and do the prereading vocabulary work for Act I. Give students the remainder of this class period to do the prereading work and, if they finish that, to begin practicing their oral reading parts.

LESSONS FOUR AND FIVE

Objectives
1. To read Act I of *Macbeth*
2. To evaluate students' oral reading

Activity
Have students who were assigned to read parts for Act I do so during these class periods. If you have not yet evaluated students' oral reading this marking period, this would be a good opportunity to do so. An Oral Reading Evaluation form is included in this unit for your convenience.

LESSON SIX

Objectives
1. To review the main events and ideas presented in Act I
2. To assign the speaking parts for Act II
3. To do the prereading work for Act II

Activity #1
Give students a few minutes to formulate answers for the study guide questions for Act I, and then discuss the answers to the questions in detail. Write the answers on the board or overhead transparency so students can have the correct answers for study purposes. Note: It is a good practice in public speaking and leadership skills for individual students to take charge of leading the discussions of the study questions. Perhaps a different student could go to the front of the class and lead the discussion each day that the study questions are discussed during this unit. Of course, the teacher should guide the discussion when appropriate and be sure to fill in any gaps the students leave.

Activity #2
Assign the following speaking parts for Act II. (Tell students that they will be reading Act II during the next class period.)

Banquo	Fleance
Macbeth	Lady Macbeth
Porter	Macduff
Lennox	Donalbain
Old Man	Ross
Narrator	

Activity #3
Prior to reading Act II, students should preview the study questions and do the prereading vocabulary work for Act II. Give students the remainder of this class period to do the prereading work and, if they finish that, to begin practicing their oral reading parts.

ORAL READING EVALUATION - *Macbeth*

Name _____ Class_____ Date _____

SKILL	EXCELLENT	GOOD	AVERAGE	FAIR	POOR
Fluency	5	4	3	2	1
Clarity	5	4	3	2	1
Audibility	5	4	3	2	1
Pronunciation	5	4	3	2	1
_____	5	4	3	2	1
_____	5	4	3	2	1

Total _____ Grade _____

Comments:

LESSON SEVEN

Objectives
1. To read Act II of *Macbeth*
2. To evaluate students' oral reading

Activity
Have students who were assigned to read parts for Act I do so during these class periods. If you have not yet evaluated students' oral reading this marking period, this would be a good opportunity to do so. An Oral Reading Evaluation form is included in this unit for your convenience.

LESSON EIGHT

Objectives
1. To give students practice writing to inform
2. To review
3. To give the teacher the opportunity to evaluate students' writing

Activity
Distribute Writing Assignment 1. Discuss the directions in detail and give students this class period to do the assignment.

Follow - Up: After you have graded the assignments, have a writing conference with the students. After the writing conference, allow students to revise their papers using your suggestions and corrections. Give them about three days from the date they receive their papers to complete the revision. I suggest grading the revisions on an A-C-E scale (all revisions well-done, some revisions made, few or no revisions made). This will speed your grading time and still give some credit for the students' efforts.

WRITING ASSIGNMENT #1 - *Macbeth*

PROMPT
Your assignment is to write a complete composition about the background information you researched at the beginning of this unit.

PREWRITING
Start by looking at the notes you took as you were gathering information. Then, look at the fact sheet you and the members of your group compiled. Think of one statement you could make about all this information. That will be the main idea of your paper. Can the information you have gathered be put into categories? (Are there some things that naturally go together?) Is there a logical progression of ideas? (Can your information be put in chronological order? If so, do it.)

DRAFTING
First write a paragraph in which you introduce the topic of your composition. The paragraphs in the body of your composition will all support or explain your main topic. The paragraphs should flow from idea to idea (from category to category, or in chronological order from earliest to latest, etc.). Your final paragraph should include the conclusions you can draw from the information presented and should bring your composition to a close.

PROMPT
When you finish the rough draft of your paper, ask a student who sits near you to read it. After reading your rough draft, he/she should tell you what he/she liked best about your work, which parts were difficult to understand, and ways in which your work could be improved. Reread your paper considering your critic's comments, and make the corrections you think are necessary.

PROOFREADING
Do a final proofreading of your paper double-checking your grammar, spelling, organization, and the clarity of your ideas.

LESSON NINE

Objectives
1. To review the main events and ideas presented in Act II
2. To assign the speaking parts for Act III
3. To do the prereading work for Act III

Activity #1
Give students a few minutes to formulate answers for the study guide questions for Act II, and then discuss the answers to the questions in detail. Write the answers on the board or overhead transparency so students can have the correct answers for study purposes.

Activity #2
Assign the following speaking parts for Act III. (Tell students that they will be reading Act III during the next class period.)

Banquo	Macbeth
Lady Macbeth	Attendant
Murderer 1	Murderer 2
Murderer 3	Servant
Lennox	Ross
Lords	Witch 1
Hecate	Narrator

Activity #3
Prior to reading Act III, students should preview the study questions and do the prereading vocabulary work for Act III. Give students the remainder of this class period to do the prereading work and, if they finish that, to begin practicing their oral reading parts.

LESSONS TEN AND ELEVEN

Objectives
1. To read Act III of *Macbeth*
2. To evaluate students' oral reading

Activity
Have students who were assigned to read parts for Act III do so during these class periods. Continue the oral reading evaluations if you have not yet given everyone in the class a grade for oral reading.

LESSON TWELVE

Objectives
1. To review the main events and ideas presented in Act III
2. To assign the speaking parts for Act IV
3. To do the prereading work for Act IV

Activity #1
Give students a few minutes to formulate answers for the study guide questions for Act III, and then discuss the answers to the questions in detail. Write the answers on the board or overhead transparency so students can have the correct answers for study purposes.

Activity #2
Assign the following speaking parts for Act IV. (Tell students that they will be reading Act IV during the next class period.)

Witch 1	Witch 2
Witch 3	Hecate
Macbeth	1st Apparition (Head)
Lennox	2nd Apparition (Bloody Child)
Lady Macduff	3rd Apparition (Crowned Child)
Ross	Son
Messenger	Murderer 1
Malcolm	Macduff
Doctor	Narrator

Activity #3
Prior to reading Act IV, students should preview the study questions and do the prereading vocabulary work for Act IV. Give students the remainder of this class period to do the prereading work and, if they finish that, to begin practicing their oral reading parts.

LESSON THIRTEEN

Objectives
1. To read Act IV of *Macbeth*
2. To evaluate students' oral reading

Activity
Have students who were assigned to read parts for Act IV do so during these class periods. Continue the oral reading evaluations if you have not yet given everyone in the class a grade for oral reading.

LESSON FOURTEEN

Objectives
    1. To review the main events and ideas presented in Act IV
    2. To assign the speaking parts for Act V
    3. To do the prereading work for Act V

Activity #1
    Give students a few minutes to formulate answers for the study guide questions for Act IV, and then discuss the answers to the questions in detail. Write the answers on the board or overhead transparency so students can have the correct answers for study purposes.

Activity #2
    Assign the following speaking parts for Act V. (Tell students that they will be reading Act V during the next class period.)

Doctor	Gentlewoman
Lady Macbeth	Menteith
Angus	Lennox
Carthness	Macbeth
Servant	Seyton
Malcolm	Siwald
Messenger	Soldiers
Macduff	Ross
Young Siward	Narrator

Activity #3
    Prior to reading Act V, students should preview the study questions and do the prereading vocabulary work for Act V. Give students the remainder of this class period to do the prereading work and, if they finish that, to begin practicing their oral reading parts.

LESSON FIFTEEN

Objectives
    1. To read Act V of *Macbeth*
    2. To evaluate students' oral reading

Activity
    Have students who were assigned to read parts for Act V do so during these class periods. Continue the oral reading evaluations if you have not yet given everyone in the class a grade for oral reading.

LESSON SIXTEEN

Objectives
    1. To review the main ideas and events from Act V
    2. To review all of the vocabulary work done in this unit

Activity #1
    Give students a few minutes to formulate answers for the study guide questions for Act V, and then discuss the answers to the questions in detail.

Activity #2
    Choose one (or more) of the vocabulary review activities listed on the next page and spend your class period as directed in the activity. Some of the materials for these review activities are located in the Extra Activities Packet in this unit.

LESSON SEVENTEEN

Objectives
    1. To give students the opportunity to practice writing to persuade
    2. To give the teacher a chance to evaluate students' individual writing
    3. To give students the opportunity to correct their writing errors and produce an error-free paper

Activity
    Distribute Writing Assignment 2. Discuss the directions in detail and give students ample time to complete the assignment.

    While students are doing their writing assignments, call individuals to your desk (or some other private area) to discuss their papers from Writing Assignment 1. A Writing Evaluation Form is included with this unit to help structure your conferences.

VOCABULARY REVIEW ACTIVITIES

1. Divide your class into two teams and have an old-fashioned spelling or definition bee.

2. Give each of your students (or students in groups of two, three or four) a *Macbeth* Vocabulary Word Search Puzzle. The person (group) to find all of the vocabulary words in the puzzle first wins.

3. Give students a *Macbeth* Vocabulary Word Search Puzzle without the word list. The person or group to find the most vocabulary words in the puzzle wins.

4. Use a *Macbeth* Vocabulary Crossword Puzzle. Put the puzzle onto a transparency on the overhead projector (so everyone can see it), and do the puzzle together as a class.

5. Give students a *Macbeth* Vocabulary Matching Worksheet to do.

6. Divide your class into two teams. Use the *Macbeth* vocabulary words with their letters jumbled as a word list. Student 1 from Team A faces off against Student 1 from Team B. You write the first jumbled word on the board. The first student (1A or 1B) to unscramble the word wins the chance for his/her team to score points. If 1A wins the jumble, go to student 2A and give him/her a definition. He/she must give you the correct spelling of the vocabulary word which fits that definition. If he/she does, Team A scores a point, and you give student 3A a definition for which you expect a correctly spelled matching vocabulary word. Continue giving Team A definitions until some team member makes an incorrect response. An incorrect response sends the game back to the jumbled-word face off, this time with students 2A and 2B. Instead of repeating giving definitions to the first few students of each team, continue with the student after the one who gave the last incorrect response on the team. For example, if Team B wins the jumbled-word face-off, and student 5B gave the last incorrect answer for Team B, you would start this round of definition questions with student 6B, and so on. The team with the most points wins!

7. Have students write a story in which they correctly use as many vocabulary words as possible. Have students read their compositions orally! Post the most original compositions on your bulletin board!

WRITING ASSIGNMENT #2 - *Macbeth*

PROMPT

We are constantly being persuaded by our friends, family members, teachers, advertisements, and many other sources. The art of persuasion is an important tool to have; if you are really good at it, you can convince most people of just about anything.

Your assignment is to practice and develop your persuasive abilities by writing a letter in which you persuade Macbeth not to kill Duncan.

PREWRITING

We can clearly see how Lady Macbeth pushes Macbeth to take action, to kill Duncan. Look at those passages in which Lady Macbeth bullies and shames Macbeth into action (particularly Act I Scene vii). Make a list of the arguments she uses.

Now, pretend you are a friend to Macbeth. You know that he has considered murdering Duncan, and you know that Lady Macbeth has been nagging him to do it. What could you say to convince Macbeth not to kill Duncan? Make a list of all the different arguments you can brainstorm. Number the items on your list in order from the best argument you have to the weakest.

There are several ways to organize your ideas. Some people prefer to work from their strongest to weakest arguments. Other people prefer to work from the weakest to the strongest. Still others prefer to start with their best and then work from their weakest to their second best arguments. Choose the organization you feel works best for the arguments you have to make and considering Macbeth is your audience.

DRAFTING

Bearing all the things you considered in the Prewriting stage in mind, write out what you would say and do to persuade Macbeth not to kill Duncan. Start with an appropriate date in your letter format. Include an appropriate salutation. Write an introductory paragraph in which you approach the topic. Write out the paragraphs in the body of your letter. (One way is to write one paragraph for each of your arguments.) Write a concluding paragraph and an appropriate closing.

PROMPT

When you finish the rough draft of your paper, ask a student who sits near you to read it. After reading your rough draft, he/she should tell you what he/she liked best about your work, which parts were difficult to understand, and ways in which your work could be improved. Reread your paper considering your critic's comments, and make the corrections you think are necessary.

PROOFREADING

Do a final proofreading of your paper double-checking your grammar, spelling, organization, and the clarity of your ideas.

WRITING EVALUATION FORM - *Macbeth*

Name _____ Date _____

Writing Assignment #1 for the *Macbeth* unit   Grade _____

Circle One For Each Item:

Grammar: correct   errors noted on paper

Spelling: correct   errors noted on paper

Punctuation: correct   errors noted on paper

Legibility: excellent   good   fair   poor

Strengths:

Weaknesses:

Comments/Suggestions:

LESSONS EIGHTEEN AND NINETEEN

Objectives
1. To examine the idea of assassinations of public leaders
2. To try to get students to understand what it would have meant to the people of Scotland to have Duncan assassinated
3. To remove the ideas in *Macbeth* from the world of the theater and bring them to a more present-day reality
4. To broaden students knowledge and understanding of a few moments in history

Activity #1

Ask your students, "Who are your heroes?" "Who do you respect?" "Who do you look up to?" "Who do you trust to give you good advice?" On the chalkboard write down the answers students give. Next, ask students how they would feel if one of the people they counted on, respected, looked up to, was suddenly assassinated--killed. Give students a chance to respond.

Transition: That's what happened to the people of Scotland when Macbeth murdered Duncan. Duncan was apparently a well-loved ruler, and the people of Scotland were to be thrown into a period of mourning and uncertainty.

Activity #2

Have students get together in small groups (4-5 students per group). Their assignment is to make a list of all the people they can think of who have been assassinated anywhere in the world at any period in history. Give students 10-15 minutes to make their lists and then have one student from each group read the group's list. Write all the students' suggestions on the board. Be prepared with a list of your own in case your students can't think of many names.

Some suggestions: Julius Caesar, President Garfield, President McKinley, President Lincoln, President Kennedy, Martin Luther King, Bobby Kennedy, Mahandas Ghandi, Indira Ghandi, Malcolm X, John Lennon, President Diem of Vietnam, Anwar Sadat, Thomas Abecket, Caliguila, Salvadore Allende, and Benigno Aquino.

Activity #3

Discuss with your students who each of the victims were, why they were assassinated, and what effect their assassinations had on the people in their countries.

Homework Assignment After Lesson Eighteen

Have students interview at least two different adults to ask for their memories of and reactions to the assassinations of JFK, Martin Luther King, and John Lennon.

Activity #4

Have students discuss the results of their interviews so that the entire class can get a feeling for the reactions of the people in our country to a few of the most recent assassinations which have greatly affected us.

Activity #5

There have been several good documentaries made about the assassinations of JFK and Martin Luther King. Show one to your students in the time that remains.

LESSON TWENTY

Objectives

    1. To discuss *Macbeth* on interpretive and critical levels
    2. To take a closer look at Shakespeare's language and significant quotations from *Macbeth*

Activity

Choose the questions from the Extra Discussion Questions/Writing Assignments which seem most appropriate for your students. A class discussion of these questions is most effective if students have been given the opportunity to formulate answers to the questions prior to the discussion. To this end, you may either have all the students formulate answers to all the questions, divide your class into groups and assign one or more questions to each group, or you could assign one question to each student in your class. The option you choose will make a difference in the amount of class time needed for this activity.

After students have had ample time to formulate answers to the questions, begin your class discussion of the questions and the ideas presented by the questions. Be sure students take notes during the discussion so they have information to study for the unit test.

EXTRA WRITING ASSIGNMENTS/DISCUSSION QUESTIONS - *MACBETH*

Interpretation

1. From what point of view is *Macbeth* written? How does that affect our perception of the play?

2. What is the setting of *Macbeth*?

3. Where is the climax of the play? Explain your choice.

4. How much time passes during the play?

5. Think of a different title for the play. Explain your choice.

6. What are the main conflicts in the play, and how are they resolved?

Critical

7. Explain the role of witches, ghosts, and visions in *Macbeth*.

8. What things motivate Macbeth?

9. Would Macbeth have killed Duncan if the witches had not predicted he would become king -- or was it truly his fate with or without the witches?

10. Evaluate William Shakespeare's style of writing. How does it contribute to the value of the play?

11. Compare and contrast Macbeth and Lady Macbeth.

12. At what point in the play is Macbeth's downfall inevitable?

13. Discuss the element of time in the play.

14. The themes/ideas of sleep and dreams recur in the play. Why?

15. Notice the light/dark imagery throughout the play. What kinds of things happen in the light? (3 examples) What kinds of things happen in the dark/storms? (3 examples)

16. In this play, the themes of nobility, bravery, honor and truth contrast sharply with the evil doings of the witches, Macbeth and Lady Macbeth. Give at least five examples of Shakespeare's use of the aforementioned themes.

Macbeth Extra Discussion Questions page 2

17. Are the characters in *Macbeth* stereotypes? If so, explain why William Shakespeare used stereotypes. If not, explain how the characters merit individuality.

18. Discuss Shakespeare's use of bells and alarms in *Macbeth*.

19. Explain the role of each: Duncan, Banquo, Malcolm, Macduff.

20. What is the use of the whole Birnam Wood episode?

Critical/Personal Response
21. Which minor character is the most important to the play? (Banquo, Macduff, Fleance, the witches, or Malcolm)

22. Did Macbeth have any redeeming qualities?

23. Would Macbeth have killed Duncan without Lady Macbeth's nagging?

24. Do you think the relationship between Macbeth and Lady Macbeth is realistic? Explain why or why not.

25. Who is responsible for Duncan's death?

26. Who is responsible for Macbeth's death?

27. Was Lady Macbeth an evil person?

Personal Response
28. Did you enjoy reading *Macbeth*? Why or why not?

29. What would you have done if you were Macbeth?

30. Suppose Banquo had lived. How would that have affected the story?

Macbeth Extra Discussion Questions page 3

Quotations
IDENTIFY AND EXPLAIN THE FOLLOWING QUOTATIONS FROM *Macbeth*.

1. Fair is foul, and foul is fair. (I.i,12)

2. Sleep shall neither night nor day
   Hang upon his penthouse lid.
   He shall live a man forbid.
   Weary sennights nine times nine
   Shall he dwindle, peak, and pine.
   Though his bark cannot be lost,
   Yet it shall be tempest-tost. (I,iii,19-25)

3. So foul and fair a day I have not seen. (I,iii,38)

4. You should be women,
   And yet your beards forbid me to interpret
   that you are so. (I,iii,45-47)

5. Good sir, why do you start, and seem to fear
   Things that do sound so fair? (I,iii 51-52)

6. Lesser than Macbeth, and greater.
   Not so happy, yet much happier.
   Thou shalt get kings, though thou be none. (I,iii,65-67)

7. Why do you dress me in borrowed robes? (I.iii,108-109)

8. And oftentimes, to win us to our harm,
   The instruments of darkness tell us truths,
   Win us with honest trifles, to betray's
   In deepest consequence. (I.iii,123-126)

9. Come what may,/Time and the hour runs through the roughest day. (I.iii,146-147)

10. Nothing in his life/ Became him like the leaving it. (I.iv,7-8)

11. There's no art/To find the mind's construction in the face. (I.iv,11-12)

12. But signs of nobleness, like stars, shall shine/on all deservers. (I.iv,41-42)

Macbeth Extra Discussion Questions page 4

13. Stars, hide your fires,/Let not light see my black and deep desires. (I.iv,50-51)

14. Glamis thou are, and Cawdor, and shalt be
    What thou art promised. Yet do I fear thy nature.
    It is too full o' the milk of human kindness
    To catch the nearest way. Thou wouldst be great,
    Art not without ambition, but without
    The illness should attend it. What thou wouldst highly,
    That wouldst thou holily -- wouldst not play false,
    And yet wouldst wrongly win. (I.v,16-23)

15. Your face, my Thane, is as a book where men/ May read strange matters. (I.v,63-64)

16. Look like the innocent flower/But be the serpent under't. (I.v,66-67)

17. Away, and mock the time with fairest show./False face must hide what the false heart doth know. (I.vii, 81-82)

18. To know my deed, 'twere best not know myself./Wake Duncan with thy knocking! I would thou couldst! (II.ii,73-74)

19. O gentle lady,/ 'Tis not for you to hear what I can speak./ The repetition, in a woman's ear, Would murder as it fell. (II.iii,88-91)

20. Had I but died an hour before this chance,
    I had lived a blessed time, for from this instant
    There's nothing serious in mortality.
    All is but toys. (II.iii,96-99)

21. There's daggers in men's smiles. (II.iii,146)

22. By the clock 'tis day,/And yet dark night strangles the traveling lamp./Is't night's predominance, or the day's shame,/That darkness does the face of earth entomb/When living light should kiss it? 'Tis unnatural,/Even like the deed that's done. (II.iv,6-11)

23. Lest our old robes sit easier than our new! (II.iv,37)

24. Naught's had, all spent,
    Where our desire is got without content,
    'Tis safer to be that which we destroy
    Than by destruction dwell in doubtful joy. (III.ii,4-7)

Macbeth Extra Discussion Questions page 5

25. Things without all remedy/Should be without regard. What's done is done. (III.ii,11-12)

26. Better be with the dead,/Whom we, to gain our peace, have sent to peace,/Than on the torture of the mind to lie/In restless ecstacy. (III.ii,19-22)

27. And make our faces vizards to our hearts,/Disguising what they are. (III.ii,33-34)

28. Things bad begun make strong themselves by ill. (III.ii,55)

29. Then comes my fit again. I had else been perfect,
    Whole as the marble, founded as the rock,
    As broad and general as the casing air.
    But now I am cabined, cribbed, confined, bound in
    To saucy doubts and fears. (III.iv,21-25)

30. I am in blood/Stepped in so far that should I wade no more,/Returning were as tedious as go o'er. (III.iv,136-138)

31. Double, double toil and trouble,/Fire burn and caldron bubble. (IV.i,10-11)

32. By the pricking of my thumbs,/Something wicked this way comes. (IV.i,44-45)

33. But I remember now
    I am in this earthly world, where to do harm
    Is often laudable, to do good sometime
    Accounted dangerous folly. Why, then, alas,
    Do I put up that womanly defense,
    To say I have done no harm? -- What are these faces? (IV.ii,74-79)

34. Angels are bright still, though the brightest fell.
    Though all things foul would wear the brows of grace,
    Yet grace must still look so. (IV.iii 22-24)

35. Oh, Scotland, Scotland! (IV.iii,100)

36. Such welcome and unwelcome things at once./'Tis hard to reconcile. (IV.iii,138-139)

37. The night is long that never finds the day. (IV.iii,240)

Macbeth Extra Discussion Questions page 6

38. Out, damned spot! Out, I say! One, two -- why, then 'tis time to do 't. Hell is murky, Fie, my lord, fie! A soldier, and afeard? What need we fear who knows it, when none can call our power to account? Yet who would have thought the old man to have had so much blood in him? . . . The Thane of Fife had a wife. Where is she now? What, will these hands ne'er be clean? No more o' that, my lord, no more o' that. You mar all with this starting. . . . Here's the smell of the blood still. All the perfumes of Arabia will not sweeten this little hand. Oh, oh, oh! (V.i,39-59)

39. To bed, to bed, there's knocking at the gate. Come, come, come, come, give me your hand. What's done cannot be undone. To bed, to bed, to bed. (V.i,73-75)

40. Those he commands move only in command,
    Nothing in love. Now does he feel his title
    Hang loose about him, like a giant's robe
    Upon a dwarfish thief. (V.ii,19-22)

41. I have lived long enough. My way of life
    Is fall'n into the sear, the yellow leaf,
    And that which should accompany old age,
    As honor, love, obedience, troops of friends,
    I must not look to have, but in their stead
    Curses, not loud but deep, mouth-honor, breath,
    Which the poor heart would fain deny, and dare not.(V.iii,22-28)

42. She should have died hereafter,
    There would have been a time for such a word.
    Tomorrow, and tomorrow, and tomorrow
    Creeps in this petty pace from day to day,
    To the last syllable of recorded time,
    And all our yesterdays have lighted fools
    The way to dusty death. Out, out, brief candle!
    Life's but a walking shadow, a poor player
    That struts and frets his hour upon the stage
    And then is heard no more. It is a tale
    Told by an idiot, full of sound and fury,
    Signifying nothing. (V.v,17-28)

43. The time is free. (V.viii,55)

LESSON TWENTY-ONE

Objectives
1. To give students the opportunity to do some creative writing with their own ideas
2. To extend students' knowledge of the characters and events in *Macbeth*
3. To give the teacher a chance to evaluate students' individual writing
4. To give students the opportunity to correct their writing errors and produce an error-free paper

Activity

Distribute Writing Assignment #3. Discuss the directions orally in detail. Allow the remaining class time for students to complete the activity.

If students do not have enough class time to finish, the papers may be collected at the beginning of the next class period.

Follow-Up: Follow up as in Writing Assignment 1, allowing students to correct their errors and turn in the revision for credit. A good time for your next writing conferences would be the day following the unit test.

WRITING ASSIGNMENT #3 - *Macbeth*

PROMPT
Let's face it. Lady Macbeth is a great character, but she'll never go down in history as anyone's sweet little ol' granny. How do you see Lady Macbeth? Is she purely evil? Is she just greedy? Is she ruthless? Does she have any sense of humor?

Your assignment is to rewrite *Macbeth* from Lady Macbeth's point of view using a first person narrative.

PREWRITING
First make a list of the events of the play in chronological order. Decide which ones Lady Macbeth would know about. Delete all others. Make any notes you can about how Lady Macbeth would view these events. Jot down phrases or comments you think she might make about each event. Choose your words and tone carefully; they will determine your characterization of Lady Macbeth.

DRAFTING
Using your notes as a guideline, write *Macbeth* from Lady Macbeth's point of view.

PROMPT
When you finish the rough draft of your paper, ask a student who sits near you to read it. After reading your rough draft, he/she should tell you what he/she liked best about your work, which parts were difficult to understand, and ways in which your work could be improved. Reread your paper considering your critic's comments, and make the corrections you think are necessary.

PROOFREADING
Do a final proofreading of your paper double-checking your grammar, spelling, organization, and the clarity of your ideas.

LESSON TWENTY-TWO

Objectives
    1. To bring the *Macbeth* unit to a close
    2. To tie together all the ideas and analyses for the unit
    3. To give students a look at the play *Macbeth* because plays are meant to be seen and heard and acted out

Activity
    The best thing to do is to take students to see a production of *Macbeth*. If however, that is impossible, find a film of the play and show it to your students. Tell students to bear in mind everything they have learned about *Macbeth* as they view the film.

    If you have students whose minds will wander instead of watching the film, tell your students to keep a little written list of things comparing and contrasting the film with your text and their expectations.

LESSON TWENTY-THREE

Objective
    To review the main ideas presented in *Macbeth*

Activity #1
    Choose one of the review games/activities included in the packet and spend your class period as outlined there. Some materials for these activities are located in the Extra Activities section of this unit.

Activity #2
    Remind students that the Unit Test will be in the next class meeting. Stress the review of the Study Guides and their class notes as a last minute, brush-up review for homework.

REVIEW GAMES/ACTIVITIES - *Macbeth*

1. Ask the class to make up a unit test for Macbeth. The test should have 4 sections: matching, true/false, short answer, and essay. Students may use 1/2 period to make the test and then swap papers and use the other 1/2 class period to take a test a classmate has devised. (open book) You may want to use the unit test included in this packet or take questions from the students' unit tests to formulate your own test.

2. Take 1/2 period for students to make up true and false questions (including the answers). Collect the papers and divide the class into two teams. Draw a big tic-tac-toe board on the chalk board. Make one team X and one team O. Ask questions to each side, giving each student one turn. If the question is answered correctly, that students' team's letter (X or O) is placed in the box. If the answer is incorrect, no mark is placed in the box. The object is to get three marks in a row like tic-tac-toe. You may want to keep track of the number of games won for each team.

3. Take 1/2 period for students to make up questions (true/false and short answer). Collect the questions. Divide the class into two teams. You'll alternate asking questions to individual members of teams A & B (like in a spelling bee). The question keeps going from A to B until it is correctly answered, then a new question is asked. A correct answer does not allow the team to get another question. Correct answers are +2 points; incorrect answers are -1 point.

4. Have students pair up and quiz each other from their study guides and class notes.

5. Give students a *Macbeth* crossword puzzle to complete.

6. Divide your class into two teams. Use the *Macbeth* crossword words with their letters jumbled as a word list. Student 1 from Team A faces off against Student 1 from Team B. You write the first jumbled word on the board. The first student (1A or 1B) to unscramble the word wins the chance for his/her team to score points. If 1A wins the jumble, go to student 2A and give him/her a clue. He/she must give you the correct word which matches that clue. If he/she does, Team A scores a point, and you give student 3A a clue for which you expect another correct response. Continue giving Team A clues until some team member makes an incorrect response. An incorrect response sends the game back to the jumbled-word face off, this time with students 2A and 2B. Instead of repeating giving clues to the first few students of each team, continue with the student after the one who gave the last incorrect response on the team. For example, if Team B wins the jumbled-word face-off, and student 5B gave the last incorrect answer for Team B, you would start this round of clue questions with student 6B, and so on. The team with the most points wins!

UNIT TESTS

SHORT ANSWER UNIT TEST 1 - *Macbeth*

I. Matching/Identify

___ 1. Duncan   A. He killed Macbeth

___ 2. Macbeth   B. Messenger who told Macduff his family was murdered

___ 3. Lady Macbeth   C. Attempted to kill Macbeth but he was slain

___ 4. Banquo   D. Encouraged Macbeth to kill Duncan

___ 5. Macduff   E. Hired murderers to kill Banquo and Fleance

___ 6. Malcolm   F. Macbeth assassinated him

___ 7. Lennox   G. His ghost appeared to Macbeth

___ 8. Ross   H. Duncan's eldest son

___ 9. Young Siward   I. Queen of the witches

___ 10. Hecate   J. One of Duncan's noblemen

II. Short Answer

1. What is the point of the first scene literally and in reference to the whole play?

2. What do the witches predict in I, iii for Macbeth? For Banquo?

3. Macbeth says, "Stars, hide your fires, Let not light see my black and deep desires." What are his desires?

Macbeth Short Answer Unit Test 1 Page 2

4. What are Macbeth's arguments to himself against killing Duncan?

5. What is Lady Macbeth's plan; how did they kill Duncan?

6. What excuse or explanation did Macbeth give for killing the guards (grooms)? What was his real reason?

7. Why do Malcolm and Donalbain leave Scotland?

8. Why does Macbeth want Banquo and Fleance dead?

9. Who (what) did Macbeth see at the banquet table?

10. What four things do the witches show Macbeth? What does each show/say?

Macbeth Short Answer Unit Test 1 Page 3

11. Why does Macbeth have Macduff's family and servants killed?

12. What trick did Malcolm use to hide the number of men in his army?

13. What is Macbeth's reaction to his wife's death?

14. How does Macbeth die?

Macbeth Short Answer Unit Test 1 Page 4

III. Quotations - Explain the significance of each of the following quotations:

1. Fair is foul, and foul is fair. (I.i,12)

2. Lesser than Macbeth, and greater.
   Not so happy, yet much happier.
   Thou shalt get kings, though thou be none. (I,iii,65-67)

3. Look like the innocent flower/But be the serpent under't. (I.v,66-67)

4. Things without all remedy/Should be without regard. What's done is done.
   (III.ii,11-12)

5. Better be with the dead,/Whom we, to gain our peace, have sent to peace,/Than on the torture of the mind to lie/In restless ecstacy. (III.ii,19-22)

6. I am in blood/Stepped in so far that should I wade no more,/Returning were as tedious as go o'er. (III.iv,136-138)

7. Oh, Scotland, Scotland! (IV.iii,100)

Macbeth Short Answer Unit Test 1 Page 5

8. Such welcome and unwelcome things at once./'Tis hard to reconcile. (IV.iii,138-139)

9. Out, out, brief candle!
   That struts and frets his hour upon the stage
   And then is heard no more. It is a tale
   Told by an idiot, full of sound and fury,
   Signifying nothing. (V.v,17-28)

Macbeth Short Answer Unit Test 1 Page 6

IV. Vocabulary

Listen to the vocabulary words and spell them. After you have spelled all the words, go back and write down the definitions.

1.

2.

3.

4.

5.

6.

7.

8.

9.

10.

KEY: SHORT ANSWER UNIT TEST #1 - *Macbeth*

I. Matching/Identify

F 1. Duncan   A. He killed Macbeth

E 2. Macbeth   B. Messenger who told Macduff his family was murdered

D 3. Lady Macbeth   C. Attempted to kill Macbeth but he was slain

G 4. Banquo   D. Encouraged Macbeth to kill Duncan

A 5. Macduff   E. Hired murderers to kill Banquo and Fleance

H 6. Malcolm   F. Macbeth assassinated him

J 7. Lennox   G. His ghost appeared to Macbeth

B 8. Ross   H. Duncan's eldest son

C 9. Young Siward   I. Queen of the witches

I 10. Hecate   J. One of Duncan's noblemen

II. Short Answer

1. What is the point of the first scene literally and in reference to the whole play?
    Literally, the witches are deciding when they shall meet again. This scene sets the mood for the entire play, and introduces several major motifs: the witches (supernatural influences in the play), the idea of fair being foul, and the stormy fate of Scotland. The main character, Macbeth, is also introduced by name.

2. What do the witches predict in I, iii for Macbeth? For Banquo?
    They predict Macbeth will be Thane of Cawdor and eventually the king. They predict that Banquo will be "lesser than Macbeth, and greater, Not so happy, and yet happier" and that his descendants will be kings although he will not be one.

3. Macbeth says, "Stars, hide your fires, Let not light see my black and deep desires." What are his desires?
    He now desires to be the king, and he realizes that something will have to be done with the present king (and his sons) before his desires can become reality.

4. What are Macbeth's arguments to himself against killing Duncan?
   Macbeth is Duncan's kinsman and his subject. Duncan is a good king and virtuous man; he has done no particular evil. Duncan is a popular king, and his death would bring sorrow and unrest upon Scotland.

5. What is Lady Macbeth's plan; how did they kill Duncan?
   She will drug the kings grooms (guards). Macbeth will then go into the king's room and murder him in his sleep.

6. What excuse or explanation did Macbeth give for killing the guards (grooms)? What was his real reason?
   He says he did it out of pain and rage, but he really wanted to eliminate any possible witnesses.

7. Why do Malcolm and Donalbain leave Scotland?
   They fear that the king's murderer will be after them, too.

8. Why does Macbeth want Banquo and Fleance dead?
   He knows they suspect him of foul play, and he is furious that he has done all of the work (so-to-speak) of becoming king, and Banquo's descendants will benefit from it.

9. Who (what) did Macbeth see at the banquet table?
   He saw Banquo's ghost.

10. What four things do the witches show Macbeth? What does each show/say?
    They showed him an armed head, a bloody child, a crowned child with a tree in its hand, and, finally, eight kings followed by Banquo's ghost. Respectively, they showed/told Macbeth to beware of Macduff, that he would not be harmed by anyone "born of woman," that he would not be vanquished until Birnam Wood would come to Dunsinane, and that Banquo's descendants would be kings.

11. Why does Macbeth have Macduff's family and servants killed?
    Macduff is not loyal to Macbeth, and Macbeth is angry.

12. Macduff says, "Oh, Scotland, Scotland!" Why?
    Malcolm has just told him what a horrid king he (Malcolm) would be if he were on the throne instead of Macbeth. Given a choice, then, between Malcolm and Macbeth, he gravely fears for his country's future.

13. What trick did Malcolm use to hide the number of men in his army?
    He has his men cut off tree branches and use them as camouflage.

14. What is Macbeth's reaction to his wife's death?
    He takes it very calmly, saying she would have died sooner or later, anyway.

15. How does Macbeth die?
    Macduff fights him and beheads him.

III. Quotations - Answers will vary depending on your class discussions.

IV. Vocabulary - Choose ten words from the vocabulary lists. Read them orally so your students can write them down for part IV of the test.

SHORT ANSWER UNIT TEST 2 - *Macbeth*

I. Matching

___ 1. Duncan   A. Hired murderers to kill Banquo and Fleance

___ 2. Macbeth   B. Queen of the witches

___ 3. Lady Macbeth   C. One of Duncan's noblemen

___ 4. Banquo   D. He killed Macbeth

___ 5. Macduff   E. Encouraged Macbeth to kill Duncan

___ 6. Malcolm   F. Messenger who told Macduff his family was murdered

___ 7. Lennox   G. Duncan's eldest son

___ 8. Ross   H. His ghost appeared to Macbeth

___ 9. Young Siward   I. Macbeth assassinated him

___ 10. Hecate   J. Attempted to kill Macbeth but he was slain

II. Short Answer

1. What do the witches predict in I.iii for Macbeth? For Banquo?

2. What arguments does Lady Macbeth use to convince Macbeth to commit the murder?

3. What is Lady Macbeth's plan?

Macbeth Short Answer Unit Test 2 Page 2

4. Macduff says, "Oh, gentle lady, 'Tis not for you to hear what I can speak. The repetition, in a woman's ear, Would murder as it fell." What is ironic about this?

5. What is Macbeth's plan for killing Banquo and Fleance? Does it work?

6. Macbeth says, "The worm that's fled Hath nature that in time will venom breed, No teeth for the present." What does that mean?

7. How does Lady Macbeth cover for Macbeth at the banquet? What excuses does she give for his wild talk?

8. What does Lennox think about Macbeth, Fleance, and Duncan's sons? Is he right?

9. Why does Macbeth have Macduff's family and servants killed?

Macbeth Short Answer Unit Test 2 Page 3

10. What does Macbeth want the doctor to do for his wife?

11. Malcolm says, "And none serve with him but constrained things Whose hearts are absent, too." What does that mean?

12. Who will be King of Scotland?

Macbeth Short Answer Unit Test 2 Page 4

III. Quotations: Explain the significance of the following quotations:

1. Sleep shall neither night nor day
   Hang upon his penthouse lid.
   He shall live a man forbid.
   Weary sennights nine times nine
   Shall he dwindle, peak, and pine.
   Though his bark cannot be lost,
   Yet it shall be tempest-tost. (I,iii,19-25)

2. Good sir, why do you start, and seem to fear
   Things that do sound so fair? (I,iii 51-52)

3. Why do you dress me in borrowed robes? (I.iii,108-109)

4. Nothing in his life/ Became him like the leaving it. (I.iv,7-8)

Macbeth Short Answer Unit Test 2 Page 5

5. Stars, hide your fires,/Let not light see my black and deep desires. (I.iv,50-51)

6. Your face, my Thane, is as a book where men/ May read strange matters. (I.v,63-64)

7. Had I but died an hour before this chance,
   I had lived a blessed time, for from this instant
   There's nothing serious in mortality.
   All is but toys. (II.iii,96-99)

8. Naught's had, all spent,
   Where our desire is got without content,
   'Tis safer to be that which we destroy
   Than by destruction dwell in doubtful joy. (III.ii,4-7)

9. Things bad begun make strong themselves by ill. (III.ii,55)

10. By the pricking of my thumbs,/Something wicked this way comes. (IV.i,44-45)

Macbeth Short Answer Unit Test 2 Page 6

11. But I remember now
   I am in this earthly world, where to do harm
   Is often laudable, to do good sometime
   Accounted dangerous folly. Why, then, alas,
   Do I put up that womanly defense,
   To say I have done no harm? -- What are these faces? (IV.ii,74-79)

12. To bed, to bed, there's knocking at the gate. Come, come, come, come, give me your hand.
    What's done cannot be undone. To bed, to bed, to bed. (V.i,73-75)

13. She should have died hereafter,
    There would have been a time for such a word.
    Tomorrow, and tomorrow, and tomorrow
    Creeps in this petty pace from day to day,
    To the last syllable of recorded time,
    And all our yesterdays have lighted fools
    The way to dusty death.

Macbeth Short Answer Unit Test 2 Page 7

IV. Vocabulary

Listen to the vocabulary words and spell them. After you have spelled all the words, go back and write down the definitions.

1.

2.

3.

4.

5.

6.

7.

8.

9.

10.

KEY: SHORT ANSWER UNIT TEST 2 - *Macbeth*

I. Matching (Use this matching key also for the Advanced Short Answer Unit Test)

__I__ 1. Duncan   A. Hired murderers to kill Banquo and Fleance

__A__ 2. Macbeth   B. Queen of the witches

__E__ 3. Lady Macbeth   C. One off Duncan's noblemen

__H__ 4. Banquo   D. He killed Macbeth

__D__ 5. Macduff   E. Encouraged Macbeth to kill Duncan

__G__ 6. Malcolm   F. Messenger who told Macduff his family was murdered

__C__ 7. Lennox   G. Duncan's eldest son

__F__ 8. Ross   H. His ghost appeared to Macbeth

__J__ 9. Young Siward   I. Macbeth assassinated him

__B__ 10. Hecate   J. Attempted to kill Macbeth but he was slain

II. Short Answer

1. What do the witches predict in I.iii for Macbeth? For Banquo?
    They predict Macbeth will be Thane of Cawdor and eventually the king. They predict that Banquo will be "lesser than Macbeth, and greater, Not so happy, and yet happier" and that his descendants will be kings although he will not be one.

2. What arguments does Lady Macbeth use to convince Macbeth to commit the murder?
    She tells him not to be a coward, not to say later that he "could have been" when he could "be" king. She tells him to be a man and go get what he wants. She says if she had made the promise to do this, that she would have killed her own baby to carry forth with her promise.

3. What is Lady Macbeth's plan?
    She will drug the kings grooms (guards). Macbeth will then go into the king's room and murder him in his sleep.

4. Macduff says, "Oh, gentle lady, 'Tis not for you to hear what I can speak. The repetition, in a woman's ear, Would murder as it fell." What is ironic about this?
   Lady Macbeth was a determining force in the death of Duncan. She is no "lady."

5. What is Macbeth's plan for killing Banquo and Fleance? Does it work?
   He gets two convicted murderers to wait along the road to ambush them. The murderers kill Banquo, but Fleance escapes.

6. Macbeth says, "The worm that's fled Hath nature that in time will venom breed, No teeth for the present." What does that mean?
   Fleance will be a problem in the future, since he will have children who will become kings, but for now Macbeth can let him go and deal with other things because Fleance is of no immediate threat to him personally.

7. How does Lady Macbeth cover for Macbeth at the banquet? What excuses does she give for his wild talk?
   She tells the guests that he often has these fits, that those who know him well have learned to ignore them. When Macbeth really gets out of hand, she sends the guests home.

8. What does Lennox think about Macbeth, Fleance, and Duncan's sons? Is he right?
   He thinks Macbeth is the "good guy," Fleance killed Banquo, and Duncan's sons killed the king. No, he is not correct.

9. Why does Macbeth have Macduff's family and servants killed?
   Macduff is not loyal to Macbeth, and Macbeth is angry.

10. What does Macbeth want the doctor to do for his wife?
    He wants the doctor to ease her suffering, to give her something to make her oblivious to her weighty troubles.

11. Malcolm says, "And none serve with him but constrained things Whose hearts are absent, too." What does that mean?
    Macbeth's armies are there in body only, not in spirit, and there should not be any serious opposition.

12. Who will be King of Scotland?
    Malcolm will be king.

III. Quotations - Answers will vary depending on your class discussions.

IV. Vocabulary - Choose ten of the vocabulary words to read orally for this section of the test.

ADVANCED SHORT ANSWER UNIT TEST - *Macbeth*

I. Matching

___ 1. Duncan   A. Hired murderers to kill Banquo and Fleance

___ 2. Macbeth   B. Queen of the witches

___ 3. Lady Macbeth   C. One of Duncan's noblemen

___ 4. Banquo   D. He killed Macbeth

___ 5. Macduff   E. Encouraged Macbeth to kill Duncan

___ 6. Malcolm   F. Messenger who told Macduff his family was murdered

___ 7. Lennox   G. Duncan's eldest son

___ 8. Ross   H. His ghost appeared to Macbeth

___ 9. Young Siward   I. Macbeth assassinated him

___ 10. Hecate   J. Attempted to kill Macbeth but he was slain

II. Composition

1. What are the main conflicts in the play, and how are they resolved?

2. Explain the role of witches, ghosts, and visions in *Macbeth*.

Macbeth Advanced Short Answer Unit Test Page 2

3. What things motivate Macbeth?

4. Compare and contrast Macbeth and Lady Macbeth.

5. Discuss the element of time in the play.

6. The themes/ideas of sleep and dreams recur in the play. Why?

Macbeth Advanced Short Answer Unit Test Page 3

7. Discuss Shakespeare's use of bells and alarms in *Macbeth*.

8. Explain the role of each: Duncan, Banquo, Malcolm, Macduff.

9. Who is responsible for Duncan's death? Why?

10. Who is responsible for Macbeth's death? Why?

Macbeth Advanced Short Answer Unit Test Page 4

III. Quotations - Explain the significance of the following quotations:

1. Fair is foul, and foul is fair. (I.i,12)

2. Lesser than Macbeth, and greater.
   Not so happy, yet much happier.
   Thou shalt get kings, though thou be none. (I,iii,65-67)

3. Stars, hide your fires,/Let not light see my black and deep desires. (I.iv,50-51)

4. O gentle lady,/ 'Tis not for you to hear what I can speak./ The repetition, in a woman's ear, Would murder as it fell. (II.iii,88-91)

5. I am in blood/Stepped in so far that should I wade no more,/Returning were as tedious as go o'er. (III.iv,136-138)

6. Oh, Scotland, Scotland! (IV.iii,100)

7. Such welcome and unwelcome things at once./'Tis hard to reconcile. (IV.iii,138-139)

Macbeth Advanced Short Answer Unit Test Page 5

8. To bed, to bed, there's knocking at the gate. Come, come, come, come, give me your hand. What's done cannot be undone. To bed, to bed, to bed. (V.i,73-75)

9. Those he commands move only in command,
   Nothing in love. Now does he feel his title
   Hang loose about him, like a giant's robe
   Upon a dwarfish thief. (V.ii,19-22)

10. I have lived long enough. My way of life
    Is fall'n into the sear, the yellow leaf,
    And that which should accompany old age,
    As honor, love, obedience, troops of friends,
    I must not look to have, but in their stead
    Curses, not loud but deep, mouth-honor, breath,
    Which the poor heart would fain deny, and dare not.(V.iii,22-28)

Macbeth Advanced Short Answer Unit Test Page 6

11. She should have died hereafter,
    There would have been a time for such a word.
    Tomorrow, and tomorrow, and tomorrow
    Creeps in this petty pace from day to day,
    To the last syllable of recorded time,
    And all our yesterdays have lighted fools
    The way to dusty death. Out, out, brief candle!
    That struts and frets his hour upon the stage
    And then is heard no more. It is a tale
    Told by an idiot, full of sound and fury,
    Signifying nothing. (V.v,17-28)

Macbeth Advanced Short Answer Unit Test Page 7

IV. Vocabulary

Listen to the vocabulary words and write them down. Go back later and write a composition in which you use all the words. The composition should relate in some way to *Macbeth*.

MULTIPLE CHOICE UNIT TEST 1 - *Macbeth*

I. Matching

___ 1. Duncan   A. Hired murderers to kill Banquo and Fleance

___ 2. Macbeth   B. Queen of the witches

___ 3. Lady Macbeth   C. One of Duncan's noblemen

___ 4. Banquo   D. He killed Macbeth

___ 5. Macduff   E. Encouraged Macbeth to kill Duncan

___ 6. Malcolm   F. Messenger who told Macduff his family was murdered

___ 7. Lennox   G. Duncan's eldest son

___ 8. Ross   H. His ghost appeared to Macbeth

___ 9. Young Siward   I. Macbeth assassinated him

___ 10. Hecate   J. Attempted to kill Macbeth but he was slain

II. Multiple Choice

1. What do the witches predict in I.iii for Macbeth? For Banquo?
    a. Macbeth will be Thane of Cawdor and eventually the king. Banquo's descendants will be king, although he will not.
    b. Macbeth will be conqueror of Norway, Banquo will be king.
    c. Macbeth will remain Thane of Glamis. Banquo will be Thane of Cawdor, neither will ever be king.
    d. Macbeth will be king. Banquo will be Thane of Glamis and Cawdor.

2. Macbeth says, "Stars, hide your fires, Let not light see my black and deep desires." What are Macbeth's desires?
    a. He wants to go home to see Lady Macbeth
    b. He wants to raise the taxes in the lands he rules
    c. He is very tired. He wants the stars to stop shining so he can sleep.
    d. He wants to be king

Macbeth Multiple Choice Unit Test 1 Page 2

3. After Lady Macbeth reads the letter, what does she tell us is her opinion of Macbeth, and how does she plan to help him?
    a. She doesn't think he would be a good king, but since he is her husband, she will support him in whatever he wants to do.
    b. She thinks he could be a good king, but he lacks the hard-heartedness which would allow him to get the position. She will talk him into it.
    c. She does not want him to be king, and vows to stop him.
    d. She thinks Banquo would be a better king, she plans to convince Macbeth to support Banquo instead.

4. What are Macbeth's arguments to himself against killing Duncan?
    a. There are too many witnesses in the castle. He could never get away with it.
    b. Macbeth is Duncan's kinsman and subject. Duncan is a good and popular king; his death would bring sorrow to Scotland.
    c. Macbeth doesn't really have the ambition to be king. He is doing this to please his wife. He may be able to change her mind.
    d. If anyone found out he did it, they would just kill him. He is better off being a Thane and being alive.

5. What arguments does Lady Macbeth use to convince Macbeth to commit the murder?
    a. She tells him not be to a coward, but to be a man and go and get what he wants.
    b. She tells him that if Duncan suspects anything and they aren't successful they will lose their lives, so he should go ahead with the plan
    c. She says that the people of Scotland will grow to love Macbeth even more than they love Duncan. He should go ahead for the good of the country.
    d. She reminds him that when they got married he promised to always make her happy, and she won't be happy until he is the king.

6. What is Lady Macbeth's plan?
    a. She will put poison in the king's food. He will die in his sleep and it will look like a natural death.
    b. They will bribe the guards and offer them money and power to kill the king.
    c. Macbeth's soldiers will come into the banquet disguised as robbers. They will commit the murder and wound Macbeth so that it doesn't look suspicious.
    d. She will drug the king's guards. Macbeth will then go into the king's room and kill him.

Macbeth Multiple Choice Unit Test 1 Page 3

7. Then, Macbeth is worried about hearing a voice saying, "Macbeth does murder sleep." What does Lady Macbeth then tell him to do?
    a. Have a glass of wine and relax
    b. Get cleaned up and forget about it
    c. Have the minstrel come and sing some quiet tunes to put them to sleep
    d. Go for a walk in the garden and get some fresh air.

8. Macduff says, "Oh, gentle lady, 'Tis not for you to hear what I can speak. The repetition, in a woman's ear, Would murder as it fell." What is ironic about this?
    a. He pretended to be brave, but he really wasn't.
    b. He sounded concerned about Lady Macbeth, but he really thought women were weak and foolish
    c. He tried to sound upset, but he was glad the king was dead.
    d. He didn't know about Lady Macbeth's part in the murder

9. Why do Malcom and Donalbain leave?
    a. They don't want to be accused of the crime.
    b. They are going to take the sad news to their mother.
    c. They are afraid the murderer will be after them, too.
    d. They want to start making the funeral arrangements.

10. Why does Macbeth want Banquo and Fleance dead?
    a. He knows they suspect him. He is furious that he has done the work to become king, and Banquo's descendants will benefit
    b. He thinks they suspect him, and that they may try to kill Lady Macbeth in retaliation.
    c. He is afraid they will try to bring Malcom and Donalbain back and make one of them king instead
    d. He has gone crazy and wants to kill anyone associated with Duncan

11. How does Lady Macbeth cover for Macbeth at the banquet?
    a. She tells the guests he often has fits. When he really gets out of hand she sends the guests home.
    b. She pretends to be ill and convinces him to go to their chambers. She asks Macduff to entertain the guests.
    c. She says he is still grieving for Duncan. She gives him wine to quiet him, and she hosts the banquet.
    d. She laughs and says he is in high spirits. She encourages the others to make merry with her and Macbeth.

Macbeth Multiple Choice Unit Test 1 Page 4

12. Which was the one thing the witches did NOT show Macbeth?
    a. A bloody child
    b. A crowned child
    c. A crying child
    d. Eight kings followed by Banquo's ghost

13. Why does Macduff says, "Oh, Scotland, Scotland?"
    a. He misses his family
    b. He fears for his country's future
    c. It is a curse against Macbeth
    d. It is a promise to be loyal to his country

14. What do the doctor and gentlewoman see Lady Macbeth doing? What do they decide to do about it?
    a. She is sleepwalking and talking about the murders. They decide to keep an eye on her, but not say anything.
    b. She is crying and tearing at her clothes. The doctor gives her something to make her sleep and tells the gentlewoman to stay close by.
    c. She is sleepwalking and calling out to Macbeth. The doctor wakes her up and then locks her in her room, with the gentlewoman on guard.
    d. She is singing and dancing. They think she is fine and they accompany her.

15. What is Macbeth's reaction to Lady Macbeth's death?
    a. He is glad, because now his secret has died with her
    b. He is calm, saying she would have died sooner or later, anyway
    c. He flies into a rage and kills the doctor
    d. He calls on the witches to bring her back to life

16. Who will be King of Scotland?
    a. Ross
    b. Macduff
    c. Malcom
    d. Siward

Macbeth Multiple Choice Unit Test 1 Page 5

III. Quotations - Identify the speaker for each quotation by matching the letter by the character's name to the appropriate quotation.

> A=Macbeth   B=Lady Macbeth   C=Macduff
> D=Donalbain E=Witch/Witches   F=Angus

1. Fair is foul, and foul is fair. (I.i,12)

2. Lesser than Macbeth, and greater.
   Not so happy, yet much happier.
   Thou shalt get kings, though thou be none. (I,iii,65-67)

3. Glamis thou are, and Cawdor, and shalt be
   What thou art promised. Yet do I fear thy nature.
   It is too full o' the milk of human kindness
   To catch the nearest way. Thou wouldst be great,
   Art not without ambition, but without
   The illness should attend it. What thou wouldst highly,
   That wouldst thou holily -- wouldst not play false,
   And yet wouldst wrongly win. (I.v,16-23)

4. Things without all remedy/Should be without regard. What's done is done.
   (III.ii,11-12)

5. I am in blood/Stepped in so far that should I wade no more,/Returning were as tedious as go o'er. (III.iv,136-138)

6. Such welcome and unwelcome things at once./'Tis hard to reconcile. (IV.iii,138-139)

7. Those he commands move only in command,
   Nothing in love. Now does he feel his title
   Hang loose about him, like a giant's robe
   Upon a dwarfish thief. (V.ii,19-22)

8. She should have died hereafter,
   There would have been a time for such a word.
   Tomorrow, and tomorrow, and tomorrow
   Creeps in this petty pace from day to day,
   To the last syllable of recorded time,
   And all our yesterdays have lighted fools
   The way to dusty death. (V.v,17-28)

Macbeth Multiple Choice Unit Test 1 Page 6

IV. Vocabulary

___ 1. SCRUPLES   A. evil; wicked

___ 2. PURGED   B. having an immoderate desire for wealth

___ 3. SURFEITED   C. one that indicates what is to come

___ 4. APPEASE   D. to bring peace

___ 5. CLEAVE   E. waits

___ 6. EQUIVOCATES   F. fills with dismay

___ 7. BIDES   G. a large vessel

___ 8. BRANDISHED   H. avoids making an explicit statement

___ 9. HARBINGER   I. the murdering of one's father, mother or relative

___10. PARRICIDE   J. an obsequious follower

___11. COURIERS   K. conscience; morals

___12. PERNICIOUS   L. special honor expressed publicly

___13. CAROUSING   M. messengers

___14. APPALL   N. extreme ill will or spite

___15. AVARICIOUS   O. drunken merrymaking

___16. CALDRON   P. to consider

___17. MALICE   Q. to adhere, cling or stick fast

___18. HOMAGE   R. to overindulge

___19. MINION   S. freed from impurities

___20. MUSE   T. waved or flourished

MULTIPLE CHOICE UNIT TEST 2 - *Macbeth*

I. Matching

___ 1. Duncan   A. Hired murderers to kill Banquo and Fleance

___ 2. Macbeth   B. Queen of the witches

___ 3. Lady Macbeth   C. One of Duncan's noblemen

___ 4. Banquo   D. He killed Macbeth

___ 5. Macduff   E. Encouraged Macbeth to kill Duncan

___ 6. Malcolm   F. Messenger who told Macduff his family was murdered

___ 7. Lennox   G. Duncan's eldest son

___ 8. Ross   H. His ghost appeared to Macbeth

___ 9. Young Siward   I. Macbeth assassinated him

___ 10. Hecate   J. Attempted to kill Macbeth but he was slain

II. Multiple Choice
1. What do the witches predict in I.iii for Macbeth? For Banquo?
    a. Macbeth will remain Thane of Glamis. Banquo will be Thane of Cawdor, neither will ever be king.
    b. Macbeth will be conqueror of Norway, Banquo will be king.
    c. Macbeth will be Thane of Cawdor and eventually the king. Banquo's descendants will be king, although he will not.
    d. Macbeth will be king. Banquo will be Thane of Glamis and Cawdor.

2. Macbeth says, "Stars, hide your fires, Let not light see my black and deep desires." What are Macbeth's desires?
    a. He wants to go home to see Lady Macbeth
    b. He wants to be king
    c. He is very tired. He wants the stars to stop shining so he can sleep.
    d. He wants to raise the taxes in the lands he rules

Macbeth Multiple Choice Unit Test 2 Page 2

3. After Lady Macbeth reads the letter, what does she tell us is her opinion of Macbeth, and how does she plan to help him?
    a. She doesn't think he would be a good king, but since he is her husband, she will support him in whatever he wants to do.
    b. She will talk him into it. She thinks Banquo would be a better king, she plans to convince Macbeth to support Banquo instead.
    c. She does not want him to be king, and vows to stop him.
    d. She thinks he could be a good king, but he lacks the hard-heartedness which would allow him to get the position.

4. What are Macbeth's arguments to himself against killing Duncan?
    a. Macbeth is Duncan's kinsman and subject. Duncan is a good and popular king; his death would bring sorrow to Scotland.
    b. There are too many witnesses in the castle. He could never get away with it.
    c. Macbeth doesn't really have the ambition to be king. He is doing this to please his wife. He may be able to change her mind.
    d. If anyone found out he did it, they would just kill him. He is better off being a Thane and being alive.

5. What arguments does Lady Macbeth use to convince Macbeth to commit the murder?
    a. She tells him that if Duncan suspects anything and they aren't successful they will lose their lives, so he should go ahead with the plan
    b. She tells him not be to a coward, but to be a man and go and get what he wants.
    c. She says that the people of Scotland will grow to love Macbeth even more than they love Duncan. He should go ahead for the good of the country.
    d. She reminds him that when they got married he promised to always make her happy, and she won't be happy until he is the king.

6. What is Lady Macbeth's plan?
    a. She will drug the king's guards. Macbeth will then go into the king's room and kill him.
    b. They will bribe the guards and offer them money and power to kill the king.
    c. Macbeth's soldiers will come into the banquet disguised as robbers. They will commit the murder and wound Macbeth so that it doesn't look suspicious.
    d. She will put poison in the king's food. He will die in his sleep and it will look like a natural death.

Macbeth Multiple Choice Unit Test 2 Page 3

7. Then, Macbeth is worried about hearing a voice saying, "Macbeth does murder sleep." What does Lady Macbeth then tell him to do?
    a. Have a glass of wine and relax
    b. Have the minstrel come and sing some quiet tunes to put them to sleep
    c. Get cleaned up and forget about it
    d. Go for a walk in the garden and get some fresh air.

8. Macduff says, "Oh, gentle lady, 'Tis not for you to hear what I can speak. The repetition, in a woman's ear, Would murder as it fell." What is ironic about this?
    a. He pretended to be brave, but he really wasn't.
    b. He sounded concerned about Lady Macbeth, but he really thought women were weak and foolish
    c. He didn't know about Lady Macbeth's part in the murder
    d. He tried to sound upset, but he was glad the king was dead.

9. Why do Malcom and Donalbain leave?
    a. They don't want to be accused of the crime.
    b. They are going to take the sad news to their mother.
    c. They want to start making the funeral arrangements.
    d. They are afraid the murderer will be after them, too.

10. Why does Macbeth want Banquo and Fleance dead?
    a. He thinks they suspect him, and that they may try to kill Lady Macbeth in retaliation.
    b. He knows they suspect him. He is furious that he has done the work to become king, and Banquo's descendants will benefit
    c. He is afraid they will try to bring Malcom and Donalbain back and make one of them king instead
    d. He has gone crazy and wants to kill anyone associated with Duncan

11. How does Lady Macbeth cover for Macbeth at the banquet?
    a. She laughs and says he is in high spirits. She encourages the others to make merry with her and Macbeth.
    b. She pretends to be ill and convinces him to go to their chambers. She asks Macduff to entertain the guests.
    c. She says he is still grieving for Duncan. She gives him wine to quiet him, and she hosts the banquet.
    d. She tells the guests he often has fits. When he really gets out of hand she sends the guests home.

Macbeth Multiple Choice Unit Test 2 Page 4

12. Which was the one thing the witches did NOT show Macbeth?
    a. A crying child
    b. A crowned child
    c. A bloody child
    d. Eight kings followed by Banquo's ghost

13. Why does Macduff say, "Oh, Scotland, Scotland?"
    a. He misses his family
    b. It is a curse against Macbeth
    c. He fears for his country's future
    d. It is a promise to be loyal to his country

14. What do the doctor and gentlewoman see Lady Macbeth doing? What do they decide to do about it?
    a. She is crying and tearing at her clothes. The doctor gives her something to make her sleep and tells the gentlewoman to stay close by.
    b. She is sleepwalking and talking about the murders. They decide to keep an eye on her, but not say anything.
    c. She is sleepwalking and calling out to Macbeth. The doctor wakes her up and then locks her in her room, with the gentlewoman on guard.
    d. She is singing and dancing. They think she is fine and they accompany her.

15. What is Macbeth's reaction to Lady Macbeth's death?
    a. He is calm, saying she would have died sooner or later, anyway
    b. He is glad, because now his secret has died with her
    c. He flies into a rage and kills the doctor
    d. He calls on the witches to bring her back to life

16. Who will be King of Scotland?
    a. Ross
    b. Siward
    c. Malcom
    d. Macduff

Macbeth Multiple Choice Unit Test 2 Page 5

III. Quotations - Identify the speaker for each quotation by matching the letter by the character's name to the appropriate quotation.

        A=Macduff   B=Witch/Witches   C=Macbeth
        D=Angus   E=Lady Macbeth   F=Donalbain

1. Fair is foul, and foul is fair. (I.i,12)

2. Lesser than Macbeth, and greater.
   Not so happy, yet much happier.
   Thou shalt get kings, though thou be none. (I,iii,65-67)

3. Glamis thou are, and Cawdor, and shalt be
   What thou art promised. Yet do I fear thy nature.
   It is too full o' the milk of human kindness
   To catch the nearest way. Thou wouldst be great,
   Art not without ambition, but without
   The illness should attend it. What thou wouldst highly,
   That wouldst thou holily -- wouldst not play false,
   And yet wouldst wrongly win. (I.v,16-23)

4. Things without all remedy/Should be without regard. What's done is done. (III.ii,11-12)

5. I am in blood/Stepped in so far that should I wade no more,/Returning were as tedious as go o'er. (III.iv,136-138)

6. Such welcome and unwelcome things at once./'Tis hard to reconcile. (IV.iii,138-139)

7. Those he commands move only in command,
   Nothing in love. Now does he feel his title
   Hang loose about him, like a giant's robe
   Upon a dwarfish thief. (V.ii,19-22)

8. She should have died hereafter,
   There would have been a time for such a word.
   Tomorrow, and tomorrow, and tomorrow
   Creeps in this petty pace from day to day,
   To the last syllable of recorded time,
   And all our yesterdays have lighted fools
   The way to dusty death. (V.v,17-28)

Macbeth Multiple Choice Unit Test 2 Page 6

IV. Vocabulary

___ 1. APPALL   A. conscience; morals

___ 2. MALICE   B. of or relating to the body

___ 3. VIZARDS   C. steadfast adherence to a strict moral code

___ 4. PURGED   D. to overindulge

___ 5. CORPORAL   E. extremely small in size

___ 6. CLEAVE   F. avoids making an explicit statement

___ 7. SCRUPLES   G. freed from impurities

___ 8. HOMAGE   H. to adhere, cling to stick fast

___ 9. BIDES   I. masks

___10. CHASTISE   J. quickly and skillfully

___11. COURIERS   K. to pass (time) pleasantly

___12. SURFEITED   L. waits

___13. DEFTLY   M. an obsequious follower

___14. INTEGRITY   N. extreme ill will or spite

___15. HARBINGER   O. one that indicates what is to come

___16. BEGUILE   P. having an immoderate desire for wealth

___17. DIMINUTIVE   Q. fills with dismay

___18. EQUIVOCATES   R. to punish

___19. MINION   S. special honor expressed publicly

___20. AVARICIOUS   T. messengers

ANSWER SHEET - *Macbeth*
Multiple Choice Unit Tests

I. Matching	II. Multiple Choice	III. Quotes	IV. Vocabulary
1. ___	1. ___	1. ___	1. ___
2. ___	2. ___	2. ___	2. ___
3. ___	3. ___	3. ___	3. ___
4. ___	4. ___	4. ___	4. ___
5. ___	5. ___	5. ___	5. ___
6. ___	6. ___	6. ___	6. ___
7. ___	7. ___	7. ___	7. ___
8. ___	8. ___	8. ___	8. ___
9. ___	9. ___		9. ___
10. ___	10. ___		10. ___
	11. ___		11. ___
	12. ___		12. ___
	13. ___		13. ___
	14. ___		14. ___
	15. ___		15. ___
	16. ___		16. ___
			17. ___
			18. ___
			19. ___
			20. ___

MULTIPLE CHOICE UNIT TESTS ANSWER KEY - Macbeth

Answers to Multiple Choice Unit Test 1 are in the left column.
Answers to Unit Test 2 are in the right column.

I. Matching	II. Multiple Choice	III. Quotes	IV. Vocabulary
1. F I	1. A C	1. E B	1. K Q
2. E A	2. D B	2. E B	2. S N
3. D E	3. B D	3. B E	3. R I
4. G H	4. B A	4. B E	4. D G
5. A D	5. A B	5. A C	5. Q B
6. H G	6. D A	6. C A	6. H H
7. J C	7. B C	7. F D	7. E A
8. B F	8. D C	8. A C	8. T S
9. C J	9. C D		9. C L
10. I B	10. A B		10. I R
	11. A D		11. M T
	12. C A		12. A D
	13. B C		13. O J
	14. A B		14. F C
	15. B A		15. B O
	16. B D		16. G K
			17. N E
			18. L F
			19. J M
			20. P P

UNIT RESOURCE MATERIALS

BULLETIN BOARD IDEAS - *Macbeth*

1. Leave a portion of the bulletin board for the students' best writing assignments.

2. Write out some of the significant quotes from the play on colorful construction paper. Cut out letters to title the board SHAKESPEARE'S *Macbeth*.

3. Take one of the word search puzzles and draw it (enlarged) on the bulletin board. Write the clue words to find to one side. Invite students to take pens and find and circle the words in the time before and after class (or perhaps if they finish their work early).

4. If your library has a picture file, look through it to find people and scenes which look like they could represent characters or scenes from *Macbeth*. Post them on colorful paper on your bulletin board. If your library (school or public) does not have a picture file, try looking in some magazines for pictures.

5. Title the board: GHOSTS, WITCHES, VISIONS AND APPARITIONS IN *Macbeth*. Draw pictures (or have your students or someone in your art department draw) pictures of all of the ghosts, witches, visions and apparitions in *Macbeth*.

6. Post articles of criticism about the play.

7. Post articles about ESP, predicting the future, or related phenomena.

8. Make a bulletin board listing the vocabulary words for this unit. As you complete sections of the play and discuss the vocabulary for each section, write the definitions on the bulletin board. (If your board is one students face frequently, it will help them learn the words.)

9. Make a bulletin board about Shakespeare and his works. Post a picture of Shakespeare in the center of your board. Post a little biography of Shakespeare under it. All around it, write the titles of all the plays he wrote or post little "playbills" for each of his plays.

10. Post a world map on your bulletin board with an enlarged map of Scotland beside it.

11. Have one of your classes do a full production of *Macbeth*. Take pictures and use them for your future bulletin boards. (Your newspaper or yearbook staff would probably be glad to take the pictures for you!)

12. Do a bulletin board about careers in politics, government and/or the military.

EXTRA ACTIVITIES

One of the difficulties in teaching literature is that all students don't read at the same speed. One student who likes to read may take the book home and finish it in a day or two. Sometimes a few students finish the in-class assignments early. The problem, then, is finding suitable extra activities for students.

The best thing I've found is to keep a little library in the classroom. For this unit on *Macbeth,* you might check out from the school library other related books and articles about castles, the history of witches, predicting the future, or the history of Scotland. Also, you might include other works by Shakespeare (either in original text or simplified versions) and articles of criticism about *Macbeth*.

Other things you may keep on hand are puzzles. We have made some relating directly to *Macbeth* for you. Feel free to duplicate them.

Some students may like to draw. You might devise a contest or allow some extra-credit grade for students who draw characters or scenes from *Macbeth*. Note, too, that if the students do not want to keep their drawings you may pick up some extra bulletin board materials this way. If you have a contest and you supply the prize (a CD or something like that perhaps), you could, possibly, make the drawing itself a non-refundable entry fee.

The pages which follow contain games, puzzles and worksheets. The keys, when appropriate, immediately follow the puzzle or worksheet. There are two main groups of activities: one group for the unit; that is, generally relating to the *Macbeth* text, and another group of activities related strictly to the *Macbeth* vocabulary.

Directions for these games, puzzles and worksheets are self-explanatory. The object here is to provide you with extra materials you may use in any way you choose.

MORE ACTIVITIES - *Macbeth*

1. Have students design a playbill for *Macbeth*.

2. Have students design a bulletin board (ready to be put up; not just sketched) for *Macbeth*.

3. Use some of the related topics (noted earlier for an in-class library) as topics for research, reports or written papers, or as topics for guest speakers.

4. Find a film version of *Macbeth*, show it, and have students evaluate it in comparison to the play.

5. Have students act out the final act of the play on your school's stage. Assign parts. Other students should work together to design the actors' costumes and the set. Lines may or may not be memorized (teacher's decision). Perhaps you could present it to another section or two of English classes during your normal class period. (Provide a background narrative for the audience.)

6. Instead of making a whole production, assign a character to each student. Have that student design his or her own costume, memorize a short passage from the play, and recite the passage (in costume) in front of the class.

7. Have an Elizabethan day in your class. Have students dress up in Elizabethan costume, play music from the period, decorate your room as a castle banquet hall, and have students each bring something for a meal of the time. This will also require some research and planning on the part of the students.

8. Spend a day with a film or slide presentation of castles in England and Scotland.

9. Find someone to give a demonstration of dueling in the times of kings and castles (or to come and speak about the history of dueling).

WORD SEARCH - *Macbeth*

All words in this list are associated with *Macbeth*. The words are placed backwards, forward, diagonally, up and down. The included words are listed below the word searches.

```
Z H B Q Z E B Y S V D X C P G K B P P F L R N J
W W L R N E N R S E R A F J E H D T C G O Z G J
M Z Y U T M G A A Z R O G S D E I G F B L D Y S
S A W A O H V N H N V P S G J M L N E L K A J L
M A C D U F F W I T C H E S E R I S E D D A E H
F E Y D Z S B L R H T H R N N R C B G N M A P C
H D B D O B I O E E T A E B T O S H A N V T T L
G L G A O N U W B A T O Z S T D I L I I I P L C
T Y S S N B W C A S N M N L Q D E S N L D K E P
T H R F L Q A A I R S C A B F R U G I N D R X K
L F U E P M U M L D D N E L I O D N A V A G N B
C G X M Y Q A O N D D X I Y C S M L C E M K K X
M G H D B L H G Q Q O C G A Z O G X P A G Y N L
S A A X G F B X H N K Y C V B N L S R B N G J H
Y L C T L X W J N O N G S Y E L E M D S F S T J
F S Y B G D W E Q N S Z C G B K A J M X K T J L
X Q Z V E D L Q B J C T F D A T R N Q L B X R C
K Y Y T Z T J S X H G P R H C P W R O T S P W V
W J J Y N W H B Q G B H S G Y F X H V D M M L P
Z S P S K R R Y P B X Y R W J Y T K R C W T Z T
```

BANQUO	ENGLAND	LENNOX	SIWARD
BELL	FLEANCE	MACBETH	SLEEP
BODY	FOUL	MACDONWALD	STARS
BRANCHES	GHOST	MACDUFF	THANE
CHILD	GLAMIS	MALCOLM	THUMB
COUSIN	HEAD	NOTHING	TIME
DAGGERS	HECATE	ROBES	TROUBLE
DAY	IRELAND	ROSS	VISIONS
DESIRES	KINGS	SCOTLAND	WITCHES
DONALBAIN	LADYMACBETH	SERPENT	
DUNCAN	LEAVING	SHAKESPEARE	

CROSSWORD - *Macbeth*

CROSSWORD CLUES *Macbeth*

ACROSS

1. Fair is _____, and _____ is fair.
4. In line for the throne after Malcolm
7. Malcolm fled to this country
10. The witches showed Macbeth a bloody _____.
12. Messenger; he told Macduff his family was murdered
13. Why do you dress me in borrowed _____?
16. Lady Macbeth's signal to Macbeth
18. King of Scotland; murdered by Macbeth
19. Macbeth is Thane of ___ and Thane of Cawdor
22. One thing drinking provokes
23. The witches showed Macbeth an armed _____.
24. Queen of witches
25. But signs of nobleness, like _____, shall shine/on all deservers.
27. _____ of Cawdor
28. The _____ is free.
29. Kills Macbeth for revenge and to restore the throne to the proper ruler
30. Macbeth had him killed because he suspected Macbeth killed Duncan
31. Macbeth defeats him, which pleases Duncan

DOWN

1. He escapes Macbeth's murder plot, but Banquo does not
2. One of Duncan's noblemen
3. There's _____ in men's smiles.
5. Macduff discovered Duncan's dead one
6. It is a table/Told by an idiot, full of sound and fury,/Signifying _____.
8. Macbeth saw Banquo's at the banquet table
9. The night is long that never finds the _____.
10. Macbeth to Duncan
11. Donalbain flees there
14. _____ Wood
15. Stars, hide your fires,/let not light see my black and deep _____.
16. Malcolm's army uses them as camouflage
17. Look like the innocent flower/But be the _____ under't.
20. Nothing is his life/Became him like the _____ it.
21. Country of which Duncan is king
22. Attempts to kill Macbeth, but he is slain
26. By the pricking of my _____, Something wicked this way comes.

CROSSWORD - *Macbeth*

	F	O	U	L				D			D	O	N	A	L	B	A	I	N
	L			E	N	G	L	A	N	D					O				O
	E			N		H		G		A		C	H	I	L	D			T
	A			N		O		G		Y		O		R		Y			H
	N		R	O	S	S		E				U		E					I
	C			X		T		R	O	B	E	S		L		D			N
B	E	L	L			S		I		I		A		E					G
R								R		N		N		S		S			
A				D	U	N	C	A	N			D		I		E			
N								A						R		R			
C						G	L	A	M	I	S		S	L	E	E	P		
H	E	A	D			E					C		I		S		E		
E				H	E	C	A	T	E		O		W				N		
S	T	A	R	S		V				T	H	A	N	E			T		
	H				T	I	M	E		L		R							
	U					N		M	A	C	D	U	F	F					
	M					G				N									
	B	A	N	Q	U	O		M	A	C	D	O	N	W	A	L	D		

MATCHING QUIZ/WORKSHEET 1 - *Macbeth*

___ 1. TIME   A. Macbeth had him killed because he suspected Macbeth killed Duncan

___ 2. DONALBAIN   B. The witches showed Macbeth a bloody _____.

___ 3. FLEANCE   C. Double, double toil and _____

___ 4. FOUL   D. It is a tale/Told by an idiot, full of sound and fury,/ Signifying _____.

___ 5. BODY   E. Nothing is his life/Became him like the _____ it.

___ 6. CHILD   F. One thing drinking provokes

___ 7. WITCHES   G. Macbeth to Duncan

___ 8. HECATE   H. Author

___ 9. KINGS   I. Hecate wants the witches to give Macbeth these false impressions

___ 10. TROUBLE   J. Hecate is their queen

___ 11. MACDUFF   K. Fair is _____, and _____ is fair.

___ 12. ROBES   L. The witches showed Macbeth eight _____.

___ 13. NOTHING   M. Kills Macbeth for revenge and to restore the throne to the proper ruler

___ 14. SHAKESPEARE   N. He escapes Macbeth's murder plot, but Banquo does not

___ 15. COUSIN   O. Macduff discovered Duncan's dead one

___ 16. DAY   P. The night is long that never finds the _____.

___ 17. VISIONS   Q. In line for the throne after Malcolm

___ 18. SLEEP   R. Queen of witches

___ 19. BANQUO   S. Why do you dress me in borrowed _____?

___ 20. LEAVING   T. The _____ is free.

KEY: MATCHING QUIZ/WORKSHEET 1 - *Macbeth*

T 1. TIME   A. Macbeth had him killed because he suspected Macbeth killed Duncan

Q 2. DONALBAIN   B. The witches showed Macbeth a bloody _____.

N 3. FLEANCE   C. Double, double toil and _____

K 4. FOUL   D. It is a tale/Told by an idiot, full of sound and fury Signifying _____.

O 5. BODY   E. Nothing is his life/Became him like the _____ it.

B 6. CHILD   F. One thing drinking provokes

J 7. WITCHES   G. Macbeth to Duncan

R 8. HECATE   H. Author

L 9. KINGS   I. Hecate wants the witches to give Macbeth these false impressions

C 10. TROUBLE   J. Hecate is their queen

M 11. MACDUFF   K. Fair is _____, and _____ is fair.

S 12. ROBES   L. The witches showed Macbeth eight _____.

D 13. NOTHING   M. Kills Macbeth for revenge and to restore the throne to the proper ruler

H 14. SHAKESPEARE   N. He escapes Macbeth's murder plot, but Banquo does not

G 15. COUSIN   O. Macduff discovered Duncan's dead one

P 16. DAY   P. The night is long that never finds the _____.

I 17. VISIONS   Q. In line for the throne after Malcolm

F 18. SLEEP   R. Queen of witches

A 19. BANQUO   S. Why do you dress me in borrowed _____?

E 20. LEAVING   T. The _____ is free.

MATCHING QUIZ/WORKSHEET 2 - *Macbeth*

___ 1. SLEEP A. King of Scotland; murdered by Macbeth

___ 2. DAGGERS B. There's _____ in men's smiles.

___ 3. DESIRES C. Country of which Duncan is king

___ 4. SIWARD D. Lady Macbeth's signal to Macbeth

___ 5. BELL E. The night is long that never finds the _____.

___ 6. ROBES F. Double, double toil and _____

___ 7. FLEANCE G. Author

___ 8. ENGLAND H. Stars, hide your fires,/let not light see my black and deep _____.

___ 9. DONALBAIN I. Macbeth to Duncan

___ 10. DAY J. Why do you dress me in borrowed _____?

___ 11. SCOTLAND K. In line for the throne after Malcolm

___ 12. VISIONS L. Macbeth is Thane of ___ and Thane of Cawdor

___ 13. LADYMACBETH M. Malcolm fled to this country

___ 14. GLAMIS N. Attempts to kill Macbeth, but he is slain

___ 15. SHAKESPEARE O. Hecate wants the witches to give Macbeth these false impressions

___ 16. KINGS P. One thing drinking provokes

___ 17. TROUBLE Q. The witches showed Macbeth eight _____.

___ 18. DUNCAN R. He escapes Macbeth's murder plot, but Banquo does not

___ 19. BANQUO S. Encourages Macbeth to kill Duncan

___ 20. COUSIN T. Macbeth had him killed because he suspected Macbeth killed Duncan

KEY: MATCHING QUIZ/WORKSHEET 2 - *Macbeth*

P   1. SLEEP   A. King of Scotland; murdered by Macbeth

B   2. DAGGERS   B. There's _____ in men's smiles.

H   3. DESIRES   C. Country of which Duncan is king

N   4. SIWARD   D. Lady Macbeth's signal to Macbeth

D   5. BELL   E. The night is long that never finds the _____.

J   6. ROBES   F. Double, double toil and _____

R   7. FLEANCE   G. Author

M   8. ENGLAND   H. Stars, hide your fires,/let not light see my black and deep _____.

K   9. DONALBAIN   I. Macbeth to Duncan

E   10. DAY   J. Why do you dress me in borrowed _____?

C   11. SCOTLAND   K. In line for the throne after Malcolm

O   12. VISIONS   L. Macbeth is Thane of __ and Thane of Cawdor

S   13. LADYMACBETH   M. Malcolm fled to this country

L   14. GLAMIS   N. Attempts to kill Macbeth, but he is slain

G   15. SHAKESPEARE   O. Hecate wants the witches to give Macbeth these false impressions

Q   16. KINGS   P. One thing drinking provokes

F   17. TROUBLE   Q. The witches showed Macbeth eight _____.

A   18. DUNCAN   R. He escapes Macbeth's murder plot, but Banquo does not

T   19. BANQUO   S. Encourages Macbeth to kill Duncan

I   20. COUSIN   T. Macbeth had him killed because he suspected Macbeth killed Duncan

JUGGLE LETTER REVIEW GAME CLUE SHEET - *Macbeth*

SCRAMBLED	WORD	CLUE
ANFCEEL	FLEANCE	He escapes Macbeth's murder plot, but Banquo does not
HECISWT	WITCHES	Hecate is their queen
GRADGSE	DAGGERS	There's _____ in men's smiles
YDA	DAY	The night is long that never finds the _____.
HICDL	CHILD	The witches showed Macbeth a bloody _____.
BESRO	ROBES	Why do you dress me in borrowed _____.
LLEB	BELL	Lady Macbeth's signal to Macbeth
ITEM	TIME	The _____ is free
ANETH	THANE	_____ of Cawdor
ILEAVGN	LEAVING	Nothing in his life/Became him like _____ it.
PRESAEKEHSA	SHAKESPEARE	Author
EPSLE	SLEEP	One thing drinking provokes
EADH	HEAD	The witches showed Macbeth an armed _____.
ANCNUD	DUNCAN	King of Scotland; murdered by Macbeth
ARDWIS	SIWARD	Attempts to kill Macbeth, but he is slain
CHEEAT	HECATE	Queen of witches
OULF	FOUL	Fair _____, and _____ is fair.
DNMCAOAWDL	MACDONWALD	Macbeth defeats him, which pleases Duncan
OTHGS	GHOST	Macbeth saw Banquo's at the banquet table
NARSHECB	BRANCHES	Malcolm's army uses them as camouflage
SSRO	ROSS	Messenger; he told Macduff his family was murdered
ELTROUB	TROUBLE	Double, double, toil and _____
SGIKN	KINGS	The witches showed Macbeth eight _____
EESRSID	DESIRES	Stars, hide your fires,/let not light see my black and deep _____
RESPTEEN	SERPENT	Look like the innocent flower/But be the _____ under't.
MUBHT	THUMB	By the pricking of _____. Something wicked this way comes.
TSRSA	STARS	But signs of nobleness, like _____, shall shine on all deservers
BM HCYTEDALA	LADY MACBETH	Encourages Macbeth to kill Duncan
NLADTSCO	SCOTLAND	Country of which Duncan is king
UBANOQ	BANQUO	Macbeth had him killed because he suspected Macbeth killed Duncan

NVISISO	VISIONS	Hecate wants to witches to give Macbeth ese false impressions
DFUFAMC	MACDUFF	Kills Macbeth for revenge and to restore the throne to the proper ruler
EOLXNN	LENNOX	One of Duncan's nobleman
LMOAMCL	MALCOLM	Duncan's eldest son
GNHITNO	NOTHING	It is a table/Told by an idiot, full of sound and fury,/Signifying _____.
OYBD	BODY	Macduff discovered Duncan's dead one

VOCABULARY RESOURCE MATERIALS

VOCABULARY WORD SEARCH - *Macbeth*

All words in this list are associated with *Macbeth* with an emphasis on the vocabulary words chosen for study in the text. The words are placed backwards, forward, diagonally, up and down. The included words are listed below.

```
Z K X N F S X Y C X Y R H D V E V P M E W Q H E
H K N S X V E Z Y O X W F V S N S T V A E P S L
I N T E G R I T Y Q R E G N I B R A H Y L U F F
F G O S D N Y Z A L F P D J P Z E H E Y M I G H
N N L I R B I M G C C S O D J L A J O P Y T C A
A F O N N W S Y O O L A R C P C R N M P R N E
W P N R P I Q Q U M V V S L A S B H D M A A M Y
J C P G D R M R R O A E I L Y L U I A S H G J Z
K T C A F L I Q P R R G P U P N Z B D S D R E Y
E M F P L E A V I U L A F R Q A D B O E T C J Y
G V Y S R S P C S S B H C X E E R L G R S I K W
X L I S U G I N P L C B N L Y A H R W B N K S C
T W N T L O E D E C C R I B N W U R I S B E P E
Q G N M U C I F E V V U U D D P R J Q C H R D N
V B S S Q N S C V F G R I P V W S L R Z I Q N W
G W J P S D I W I E T S W B L B Q G M N W D S K
S F V R W N N M B N H L K B L E L B C L N R E Z
Y S S Z H K V S I E R G Y S F L S C F L B R W J
K P H G S G M C D D D E Y J M K L R J G N D J Y
I N T E R D I C T I O N P N V Z T K N W W S Q M
```

AGUE	CAROUSING	EQUIVOCATES	PALPABLE
APPALL	CENSURES	HARBINGER	PARRICIDE
APPEASE	CHASTISE	HOMAGE	PERNICIOUS
AVARICIOUS	CLEAVE	INTEGRITY	PURGED
BEGUILE	CORPORAL	INTERDICTION	SCRUPLES
BIDES	COURIERS	MALICE	SUBORNED
BRANDISHED	DEFTLY	MINION	VIZARDS
CALDRON	DIMINUTIVE	MUSE	

VOCABULARY CROSSWORD - *Macbeth*

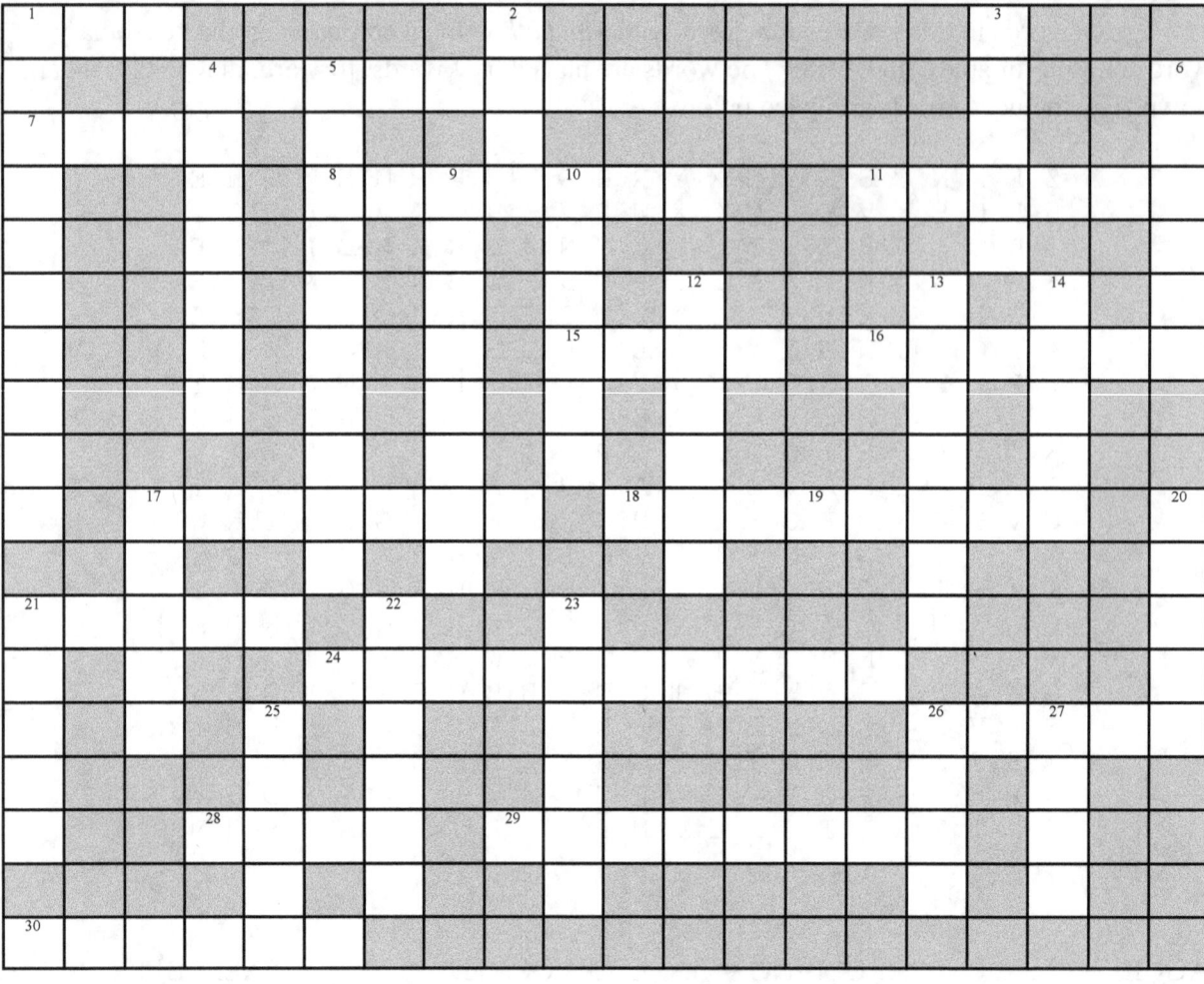

ACROSS
1. The night is long that never finds the _____.
4. Waved or flourished
7. To consider
8. To bring peace
11. Special honor expressed publicly
15. A chill or fit of shivering
16. Extreme ill will or spite
17. double, double toil and _____
18. Harsh criticisms
21. But signs of nobleness, like _____, shall shine/on all deservers.
24. Evil; wicked
26. Why do you dress me in borrowed _____?
28. Fair is _____, and _____ is fair.
29. Messengers
30. Queen of witches

DOWN
1. Extremely small in size
2. The _____ is free.
3. By the pricking of my _____, Something wicked this way comes.
4. To pass (time) pleasantly
5. Having an immoderate desire for wealth
6. To adhere, cling or stick fast
9. Easily perceived
10. Fills with dismay
12. Freed from impurities
13. A large vessel
14. Waits
17. _____ of Cawdor
19. Conscience; morals
20. The witches showed Macbeth eight _____.
21. One thing drinking provokes
22. Quickly and skillfully
23. An obsequious follower
25. Macbeth saw Banquo's at the banquet table
26. Messenger; he told Macduff his family was murdered
27. Macduff discovered Duncan's dead one

VOCABULARY CROSSWORD ANSWER KEY - *Macbeth*

								T						T			
D	A	Y															
I				B	R	A	N	D	I	S	H	E	D			H		C
M	U	S	E		V		M									U		L
I			G		A	P	P	E	A	S	E			H	O	M	A	G	E
N			U		R		A		P						B		A
U			I		I		L		P		P			C		B		V
T			L		C		P	A	G	U	E		M	A	L	I	C	E
I			E		I		A		L		R			L		D		
V					O		B		S		G			D		E		
E		T	R	O	U	B	L	E		C	E	N	S	U	R	E	S		K
		R			S		E				D			O					I
S	T	A	R	S		D			M					N					N
L		N		P	E	R	N	I	C	I	O	U	S						G
E		E		G		F			N					R	O	B	E	S
E				H		T			I					O		O		
P			F	O	U	L		C	O	U	R	I	E	R	S		D	
			S		Y			N						E		Y		
H	E	C	A	T	E													

VOCABULARY WORKSHEET 1 - *Macbeth*

_____ 1. CENSURES   A. Avoids making an explicit statement

_____ 2. CHASTISE   B. An obsequious follower

_____ 3. DEFTLY   C. Special honor expressed publicly

_____ 4. CAROUSING   D. Waits

_____ 5. BIDES   E. To adhere, cling or stick fast

_____ 6. MALICE   F. To punish

_____ 7. SUBORNED   G. Drunken merrymaking

_____ 8. EQUIVOCATES   H. Quickly and skillfully

_____ 9. INTEGRITY   I. Induced to commit an unlawful act

_____ 10. VIZARDS   J. Extreme ill will or spite

_____ 11. HOMAGE   K. Easily perceived

_____ 12. CORPORAL   L. Steadfast adherence to a strict moral code

_____ 13. AGUE   M. Of or relating to the body

_____ 14. APPEASE   N. To forbid authoritatively

_____ 15. CLEAVE   O. To bring peace

_____ 16. PERNICIOUS   P. Masks

_____ 17. INTERDICTION   Q. Harsh criticisms

_____ 18. PARRICIDE   R. Evil; wicked

_____ 19. MINION   S. A chill or fit of shivering

_____ 20. PALPABLE   T. The murdering of one's father, mother or relative

KEY: VOCABULARY WORKSHEET 1 - *Macbeth*

Q	1. CENSURES	A. Avoids making an explicit statement
F	2. CHASTISE	B. An obsequious follower
H	3. DEFTLY	C. Special honor expressed publicly
G	4. CAROUSING	D. Waits
D	5. BIDES	E. To adhere, cling or stick fast
J	6. MALICE	F. To punish
I	7. SUBORNED	G. Drunken merrymaking
A	8. EQUIVOCATES	H. Quickly and skillfully
L	9. INTEGRITY	I. Induced to commit an unlawful act
P	10. VIZARDS	J. Extreme ill will or spite
C	11. HOMAGE	K. Easily perceived
M	12. CORPORAL	L. Steadfast adherence to a strict moral code
S	13. AGUE	M. Of or relating to the body
O	14. APPEASE	N. To forbid authoritatively
E	15. CLEAVE	O. To bring peace
R	16. PERNICIOUS	P. Masks
N	17. INTERDICTION	Q. Harsh criticisms
T	18. PARRICIDE	R. Evil; wicked
B	19. MINION	S. A chill or fit of shivering
K	20. PALPABLE	T. The murdering of one's father, mother or relative

VOCABULARY WORKSHEET 2 - *Macbeth*

_____ 1. PARRICIDE   A. One that indicates what is to come

_____ 2. APPALL   B. Fills with dismay

_____ 3. BIDES   C. Extremely small in size

_____ 4. COURIERS   D. Waved or flourished

_____ 5. VIZARDS   E. A chill or fit of shivering

_____ 6. MALICE   F. Easily perceived

_____ 7. BRANDISHED   G. To punish

_____ 8. CHASTISE   H. Waits

_____ 9. INTERDICTION   I. A large vessel

_____ 10. DIMINUTIVE   J. Having an immoderate desire for wealth

_____ 11. CLEAVE   K. To forbid authoritatively

_____ 12. MINION   L. An obsequious follower

_____ 13. APPEASE   M. Extreme ill will or spite

_____ 14. PALPABLE   N. Messengers

_____ 15. AVARICIOUS   O. The murdering of one's father, mother or relative

_____ 16. MUSE   P. Masks

_____ 17. CENSURES   Q. To bring peace

_____ 18. CALDRON   R. To adhere, cling or stick fast

_____ 19. HARBINGER   S. Harsh criticisms

_____ 20. AGUE   T. To consider

KEY: VOCABULARY WORKSHEET 2 - *Macbeth*

O	1. PARRICIDE	A. One that indicates what is to come
B	2. APPALL	B. Fills with dismay
H	3. BIDES	C. Extremely small in size
N	4. COURIERS	D. Waved or flourished
P	5. VIZARDS	E. A chill or fit of shivering
M	6. MALICE	F. Easily perceived
D	7. BRANDISHED	G. To punish
G	8. CHASTISE	H. Waits
K	9. INTERDICTION	I. A large vessel
C	10. DIMINUTIVE	J. Having an immoderate desire for wealth
R	11. CLEAVE	K. To forbid authoritatively
L	12. MINION	L. An obsequious follower
Q	13. APPEASE	M. Extreme ill will or spite
F	14. PALPABLE	N. Messengers
J	15. AVARICIOUS	O. The murdering of one's father, mother or relative
T	16. MUSE	P. Masks
S	17. CENSURES	Q. To bring peace
I	18. CALDRON	R. To adhere, cling or stick fast
A	19. HARBINGER	S. Harsh criticisms
E	20. AGUE	T. To consider

VOCABULARY JUGGLE LETTER REVIEW GAME CLUES - *Macbeth*

SCRAMBLED	WORD	CLUE
PAEAPES	APPEASE	to bring peace
UEAG	AGUE	a chill or fit of shivering
VEAECL	CLEAVE	to adhere, cling or stick fast
IHNDSEABDR	BRANDISHED	waved or flourished
RSUNBDOE	SUBORNED	induced to commit an unlawful act
GRPDUE	PURGED	freed from impurities
EPICDIRRA	PARRICIDE	the murdering of one's father, mother or relative
SNEUESRC	CENSURES	harsh criticisms
IRBEHGRAN	HARBINGER	one that indicates what is to come
RROOLACP	CORPORAL	of or relating to the body
OCQVEUTSAIE	EQUIVOCATES	avoids making an explicit statement
YFELDT	DEFTLY	quickly and skillfully
ZDISAVR	VIZARDS	masks
OIVIAAUCSR	AVARICIOUS	having an immoderate desire for wealth
DEIUTRESF	SURFEITED	to overindulge
RLOADNC	CALDRON	a large vessel
ENOPRIUCSI	PERNICIOUS	evil; wicked
IBSDE	BIDES	waits
ESUM	MUSE	to consider
ITGTNIYRE	INTEGRITY	steadfast adherence to a strict moral code
ONGUSICAR	CAROUSING	drunken merrymaking
ALPLPA	APPALL	fills with dismay
AIELMC	MALICE	extreme ill will or spite
NIITVDEMIU	DIMINUTIVE	extremely small in size
UISEROCR	COURIERS	messengers
EUBILEG	BEGUILE	to pass (time) pleasantly
SASHETCI	CHASTISE	to punish
APPLEBAL	PALPABLE	easily perceived
NNOIMI	MINION	an obsequious follower
ENIOCTITNDIR	INTERDICTION	to forbid authoritatively
AEHGOM	HOMAGE	special honor expressed publicly

www.ingramcontent.com/pod-product-compliance
Lightning Source LLC
Chambersburg PA
CBHW051410070526
44584CB00023B/3371